Leaves on the Line

Leaves on the Line

Letters on Trains to
The Daily Telegraph

Edited by
Gavin Fuller

First published 2012 by
Aurum Press Ltd
7 Greenland Street
London NW1 0ND
www.aurumpress.co.uk

ISBN 978 1 84513 776 2

10 9 8 7 6 5 4 3 2 1
2016 2015 2014 2013 2012

Typeset in Mrs Eaves and Gill Sans by SX Composing DTP, Rayleigh, Essex
Printed by the MPG Books Group

FOREWORD

How do you deal with someone who insists on cutting his fingernails in a crowded carriage? Telegraph readers never fail in the ingenuity with which they approach the unforeseen hazards of railway travel. Why, asked one curmudgeon in 1935, are women such a nuisance in smoking carriages, forever opening the window for air? The problem in 2002 was mobile phones. Solutions proposed in reply included reading *The Daily Telegraph* aloud in competition, and taking a close and open interest in the mobile conversation, nodding, smiling and cupping the ear for every word.

The remarkable mastery of railway lore by letter-writers entertains as it informs, in an admirably Reithian way. In 1932, a Leeds clergyman (one of the keenest railway professions) remembered travelling on the nine-mile monorail from Listowel to Ballybunion. This extraordinary design, which had the trains straddling a single raised rail, was said to have required careful balancing, so that a farmer who sent a cow to market would have to send a couple of calves with it for the sake of stability.

Contrariwise, how many travellers today appreciate that even by 1935 railway timetables had still not adopted the 24-hour clock, wallowing instead in a confusion of a.m. and p.m.? And it remains surprising to realise that Whitstable, the home of the 'native' oyster, possessed a railway in 1830, before ever one was built for the convenience of Londoners or Mancunians.

Gavin Fuller's bright and quirky selection of railway letters to the editor is not of interest to gricers and rivet-counters alone. The train stands for all human life. Its arrival and performance never fail to attract informed and heated comment. Sometimes these verge on the metaphysical. Where, one reader inquired in 2008, is Ebbsfleet? His investigations had found only that the station was in a featureless muddy field. Yet there is a stage beyond the metaphysical: the absurd. No announcement, surely, could be more Kafkaesque and useless than that frequently heard last year by a reader at Faversham (where the train divides, one half going on to Dover, the other half to Ramsgate): 'This,' the disembodied voice assured passengers, 'is coach number eleven of eight.'

Christopher Howse
Letters Editor, *Daily Telegraph*

'OLDEST RAILWAY TUNNEL'
Leicester or Whitstable?

SIR — I see from a paragraph in *The Daily Telegraph* of Sept. 20 that passenger traffic through Glenfield Tunnel, near Leicester, is to cease.

It would appear, however, that there is a misapprehension in stating that this tunnel is the oldest in the world, unless it was completed considerably earlier than the actual opening of the Leicester and Desford line in 1832. There is a tunnel in this country which dates back earlier than this, through which a regular passenger train service passes daily, Sundays included. I refer to Tyler Hill Tunnel, situated on what was originally the Canterbury and Whitstable Railway, now the Whitstable Harbour branch of the Southern Railway. This line was opened for traffic on May 3, 1830, and was the second public railway in England, the Stockton and Darlington Railway having been opened in September, 1825. The home of the 'native', therefore, had railway facilities before Liverpool, Manchester, or London; as a matter of fact, the better-known railway joining the two former cities was opened five months after the Whitstable line.

Tyler Hill Tunnel, which is nearly half a mile in length, is of such diminutive bore that passenger trains built to present-day loading gauges cannot pass through it. Before the engines and carriages at present in use on the line could be put into service there their height had to be reduced by about eighteen inches. Before this was done only the most antiquated rolling stock could be used on the branch.

Therefore, besides being older than Glenfield Tunnel,

the tunnel at Tyler Hill shares with it the distinction of having one of the smallest bores driven for a standard-gauge line in this country.

E.S. Groves
Harrow

SIR – The correspondent who mentions the tunnel on the Leicester and Swannington line as the oldest railway tunnel in the world is, I think, slightly in error. The Leicester and Swannington Railway was opened in 1832, whereas on May 3, 1830, the Canterbury and Whitstable Railway was opened, and this had a tunnel upon it, which, according to fable, was incorporated by the proprietors in order that they might have the honour of owning the first railway tunnel in the world. For many years its small dimensions have accounted for the use of antiquated rolling stock of restricted size on this branch of the South-Eastern Railway.

Charles F. Klapper
Bow, E3

26 SEPTEMBER 1928

'RESTORE SECOND CLASS'

SIR – I was interested in the article which appeared in last Thursday's issue of *The Daily Telegraph* on the subject of 'Third-Class Sleepers'. You mention that 'the English railways are in fact providing for third-class passengers precisely similar comfort to that which the French companies offer only to the first-class fares'. I have been travelling recently in Northern France with my family and we make a point of travelling always third class, as we are thus able to see and do a great deal more with the resources at our disposal.

What struck me was that in France the railway passenger has a choice which is not open to him in this country. If he desires a certain amount of comfort he can travel second class, if luxury first class. If he chooses to dispense with either he can put up with wooden seats, which are so rounded as not to be really uncomfortable. Some of the carriages have leather seats with wooden backs. The point, however, is that one can travel third class in France for (I think I am right in saying) about one-third of third-class fare in this country. Here comfort is provided for all, and we pay for it.

I have been wondering what would be the effect of restoring second-class compartments on our railways and providing less luxurious third-class compartments at lower charge.

E.A.H. Jay
The Athenæum, SW1

26 OCTOBER 1932

STORY OF A FORGOTTEN LINE

SIR — The query raised as to the identity of the 'P.S. and N.W. Railway' by the contributor of the article on railway ticket collecting recalls one of the romances of railway history. The Potteries, Shrewsbury, and North Wales Railway was intended to join the Great Northern system to Porth Dynllyn in Carnarvonshire, and give the G.N.R. a short sea route from King's Cross and the Midlands to Ireland.

Only the section from Shrewsbury to Llanymynech was opened, laid out most expensively as a double track main line, with easy curves and gradients and a massive bridge over the Severn. This small section was not remuneratively operated and was closed down in 1880.

In 1904 a railway historian raided a booking office and secured tickets and timetables, &c., for preservation. By that time weeds covered the course, bridges and buildings had collapsed, and there seemed no likelihood of revival.

But in 1911 Lt.-Col. H.F. Stephens, the well-known light railway engineer, reconstructed the line to supply local needs. The inquiring traveller can journey to-day over the Shropshire and Montgomeryshire Railway in a petrol railcar to view a pleasing countryside.

Charles F. Klapper
London, E3

THE LAST TRAIN

SIR – I have in my possession a first-class return ticket of the P.S. and N.W. Railway for use between Shrewsbury and Llanymynech. At one time I had one of the wagon books and several other tickets. One of them was an excursion ticket from Shrewsbury to Nesscliffe, and had printed on it as an extra inducement to would-be travellers 'closed carriages'.

The old railway guard used to tell the story that when the receivers came to take possession of the line, the driver took the last train to the foot of the Briedden Hills, unhooked the engine, and left the carriages and their occupants stranded.

During the years that the railway was derelict, between 1880 and 1911, the rails, station building and bridges were left, as well as an odd signal here and there and one signal cabin with levers. At Kinnerley there was left standing one truck, which stood on the rails, and was used again when the line was reconstructed. In my childhood it was a favourite pastime to borrow a trolley belonging to a former guard and travel up the line, which was overgrown with grass and wild flowers.

R.H. Mortis
Hertford

28 OCTOBER 1932
THE 'POTTS'

SIR – It has been most interesting to read of the Potteries, Shrewsbury and North Wales Railway. Its present-day successor, the Shropshire and Montgomeryshire Railway, still referred to familiarly as the 'Potts', runs at the rear of my house. Passenger traffic nowadays is very small, but there are still two trains a day to Llanymynech and one a week on the small Breidden, or Criggion, branch.

This line crosses the Severn by a most interesting wooden pile bridge at Melverley. The granite traffic from the Breidden is very considerable. Visitors to Shropshire would find a trip on the 'Potts' well worth while.

W.E. Medlicott, Shrewsbury

'L. AND B. LATIGUE RAILWAY'

SIR – In your article on 'Old Railway Mysteries' mention is made of the 'L. and B. Latigue Railway'. Is not this the mono-rail branch which used to run, and may still do so, from Listowel to Ballybunion, in Ireland? I travelled on it in 1902, going from Killarney on purpose to do so.

(Rev.) R.H. Harvey
Leeds

SIR – The Listowel and Ballybunion Railway, Co. Kerry, was opened on March 1, 1888. Its track was nine miles long, and it had three locomotives, five passenger vehicles and forty-five goods vehicles. It was worked on the mono-rail system – a raised single rail with the carriages fitting groove-like upon it.

W. Bruce Binns
Walsall

20 JANUARY 1933

IS UNIFICATION THE SOLUTION?

SIR – The railway companies, having accepted the finding of the independent chairman of the National Wages Board on their application for a reduction in wages and salaries, must now look in other directions for means to assist in restoring their waning fortunes.

The Government as a consequence is being urged immediately to announce its decision on the far-reaching proposals made in the report of the Salter Conference. It is inferred in some quarters that to implement this report is now the only practicable step. But may I point out that if those recommendations were adopted in their entirety it is not likely that the net revenue of the railways would be materially improved?

The position of the railways is admittedly serious, but in my view it is still possible to secure for them a satisfactory future. At least two major factors must be taken into con - sideration – the redundancy of the railway facilities at present offered, and the question of the capital accounts of the companies.

With regard to the first point, the companies have already made some progress.

There are, however, still four main-line railway companies, each a distinct entity and concerned as to its own position. In these circumstances not only does over-capitalisation remain, but strict limits are set to the extent to which economies can be carried out. Moreover, each has its own head office organisation, locomotive works, carriage building, and other expensive departments.

With the ground thus prepared, the suggestion may be advanced that a new authority should be created by Act of Parliament, under the title of the Railway Transport Authority, or some other suitable title, to take over the four main-line railway companies. Under this scheme there would be a Board of perhaps nine men of proved capacity to manage the existing main-line railways as a single system.

The necessity for some such scheme was recognised soon after the war, and a considerable step was taken by the Railways Act, 1921. But having regard to the present position it may be submitted that the time has arrived for complete unification. If partial unification was right in principle ten or twelve years ago, then there is a good case now for carrying the principle to its logical conclusion.

John F. Heaton (Chairman of Thomas Tilling Ltd)
Westminster, SWı

23 JANUARY 1933

SIR – Mr John F. Heaton, chairman of Thos. Tilling Ltd., in *The Daily Telegraph* to-day urges complete unification of the main-line railways as a solution to their difficulties. He appears to put this forward as an alternative to the adoption of the Salter Report.

That report contains the unanimous recommendations of

a conference consisting of both road and rail representatives on measures to establish a fair basis of competition between the two transport agencies. That is a broad question of justice which stands by itself, and neither unification nor a proper settlement of the wages question can be regarded as an alternative solution of the competitive problem. The Salter Report should be adopted whether the railways continue as at present, or are unified under one control, as Mr Heaton suggests.

Apart from this aspect, it would be an intolerable injustice to railway stock holders if their stocks were to be valued for conversion purposes at the depressed market prices now ruling. Obviously, an adjustment would have to be made to allow for depreciation in value of railway stocks caused by competition from road transport operating under unfair and subsidised conditions. The first, and the immediate, step is that the conditions of competition between rail and road should be made equitable.

Lt-Cmdr Aubrey F. Inglefield,
Hon. Secretary, British Railway Stockholders' Union
London, WC2

25 JANUARY 1933

SIR – It is apparent that Cmdr Inglefield is labouring under a common misunderstanding in attaching too much importance to the nominal amount of stock that might be allotted to existing stockholders. In the case of many prosperous companies stock is issued of no par value. The all-important consideration for stockholders, and the one which will fix the future value of their stock, is that of income.

8

Under the scheme I have put forward in *The Daily Telegraph* large savings would be effected by the cutting out of redundant facilities, the closing down of departments which would then be superfluous, and the natural reduction in overhead charges which would also follow. All this would be to the obvious advantage of the existing stockholders, who would have exchanged their present holdings for stock of the proposed Railway Transport Authority.

May I also briefly reply to the Commander's remarks on the Salter Report? I have every sympathy with the railway stockholders, but in my view the recommendations of the committee, if carried out, would not help them in any material way. On the other hand, I believe that under my proposals the stockholders would gain substantially both in capital and income.

J.F. Heaton (Chairman of Thomas Tilling Ltd)
Westminster, SW1

26 JANUARY 1933

SIR – Mr Heaton may or may not be right when he claims that railway unification would result in economies, and therefore in an increased return in capital. But his proposals cannot be regarded as an alternative to the Salter Report, the object of which is to establish equitable conditions of competition between rail and road goods transport.

Would Mr. Heaton confine his scheme to unification of the railways? He is familiar with the control of large-scale undertakings engaged in passenger road transport. There are at present some 6,400 owners of public service vehicles in this country, of whom 2,700 own only one vehicle each. Would Mr Heaton say that unification is desirable here, and in the case also of road hauliers whose numbers are legion but unknown?

I suggest that Mr Heaton might look further afield and consider the proper co-ordination of all inland transport agencies. The Salter Conference has rightly claimed that the adoption of its recommendations is a necessary antecedent to that end.

Lt-Cmdr Aubrey F. Inglefield
Hon. Sec., British Railway Stockholders' Union
London, WC2

18 JUNE 1935
EASY TRAIN-FINDING

SIR — I have just spent some unpleasant minutes ploughing through the confusion of a railway guide, with its irritating a.m. and p.m. Surely it is time these encyclopædic time-tables simplified matters for themselves and their users by working on the 24-hour system?

The same firm publishes an air guide based on the 24-hour clock which is a model of clarity and simplicity.

There are 24 hours in the day. It follows from this that the best way to label the hours of the day is to number them 1 to 24 straight through. Any other scheme is evidence of a warped mentality.

Horæ Simplicitæ
Rock Ferry, Cheshire

24 JUNE 1935
24-HOUR TIME-TABLES

SIR – May I be allowed to endorse the remarks made by 'Horæ Simplicitæ' on railway time-tables? I have just returned from a tour of several European countries, and, although I know no foreign language and am quite ignorant of all matters 'foreign', I found no difficulty in reading correctly their time-tables, which are models of clarity and simplicity. They are all, of course, based on the 24-hour clock.

I realise that we in England are rather slow to grasp a new idea but surely the advantages of adopting time-tables based on the 24-hour clock should be obvious to everyone.

Wanderer, Hampstead

SIR – The request of your correspondent 'Horæ Simplicitæ' for a 24-hour railway time-table is not untimely. Many would be willing to pay an extra price for its simplicity.

The only people who found it difficult during the recent B.B.C. experiment were those who attempted to translate it to 12-hour time and did not endeavour to think in 24-hour time.

W.H. Sanders
Barfield Road, Leytonstone

13 DECEMBER 1935
FOR MEN ONLY
'A Crying Need' upon the Railways

SIR – I beg of you, as the editor of a newspaper fit for heroes (as opposed to heroines), to aid me in a campaign for the benefit of Man (as opposed to Woman). I refer to the crying need, on our railways, of carriages reserved for Men Only.

I observe that women hate each other so intensely that they will not willingly travel in the same railway carriage with each other. Arriving at a London terminus every evening some 10 minutes before my train leaves, I find one corner in every smoking carriage occupied by a woman. She faces the engine, and she is invariably a non-smoker.

As soon as the male pipes and what-not are burning well she opens the window, and we are all subjected to fierce draughts to which she, swathed in fur, is insensible. Someone taught these females, when they were 'but little children weak', that fresh air was good for you, and they believe it as firmly as they believe everything except our reasons for working late.

I have puffed pipe smoke over them until I have burned my tongue; I have bought the cigars advertised in your pages in an endeavour to smoke them out, but, bless you, they like cigar smoke — it is so utterly non-female.

I have ostentatiously turned up my collar and reached my hat from the rack, I have made pointed remarks as to my bald head, and I have wrapped my paper round my legs, but all to no purpose.

I am no hater of women. I shall always have as many wives as the law allows. But I hold that womankind, like fresh air, should be kept strictly in its place. In this instance, outside the window of a smoking carriage.

Lionel Mundy,
Great Castle Street, W1

14 DECEMBER 1935

SIR — The exasperating behaviour of non-smoking women

who travel in smoking compartments has become so general that businessmen find the daily train journey an intolerable nuisance.

If the railways must segregate the sexes, why not be fair and provide compartments for men only, as your correspondent Mr Lionel Mundy suggests.

It would be better still, of course, to do away with antiquated restrictions.

Reginald Arkell
Henrietta Street, WC

SIR – It is usually my personal endeavour to find accommodation in a 'non-smoking' compartment, but in nine cases out of ten the majority of persons in this compartment are men.

Women are well aware that there is usually much more available room in a smoking compartment, and that is probably the only place where they can get a seat.

(Mrs) D.E. Line
London, W1

SIR – I think that what your correspondent Mr Mundy really wants is that the railways should provide carriages with windows that cannot be opened.

I am a heavy smoker, but I always travel in a non-smoking carriage for the simple reason that when half a dozen pipes (usually foul) are being smoked and the windows are shut the atmosphere is suffocating.

H.W. Dunlacher
Bishopsgate, EC2

16 DECEMBER 1935

SIR – Why do women occupy the four corners of smoking carriages? Because more often than not the four corners of the non-smoking carriages are occupied by men who, in nine cases out of ten, light up their pipes or cigarettes as soon as the train reaches the station at which they wish to alight, thus proving that they are not occupying these carriages because they object to smoking.

Why is it that men try to make things as uncomfortable as possible for women who travel daily to the city? Last night I travelled on the District line when a crusty male entered the carriage, and although there was ample room in the carriage, insisted on sitting practically on my lap. Every time I turned over the pages of my paper he glared at me because I was forced to dig my elbows into his ribs. This is not an isolated instance of men's incredible selfishness when travelling.

We don't like either cigar or pipe smoke puffed in our faces. Let men be kippered; we prefer the fresher air of the non-smokers – when we can get into them.

(Miss) Agnes M. Abney
Kew Gardens, Surrey

SIR – You ridiculous, selfish male, surely you have the following alternatives:

1. Sit on the other side of the carriage;
2. Travel first-class;
3. Ask the lady to close the window (nicely, of course);
4. Buy a new pipe (old ones smell);
5. Walk;

and, you naughty, rude boy, to blow your horrible, filthy smoke in the lady's face. No wonder she kept the window open – Bah!

Considerate Smoker
Greenford, Middlesex

SIR – As a woman I welcome Mr Lionel Mundy's letter and accept his suggestion with enthusiasm. By all means let the heroes have their own carriages, plainly marked as such.

I am a smoker; I dislike open windows in cold weather, but I instinctively make for a non-smokers' compartment because of the repulsive brands of tobacco that most men I meet in trains appear to smoke. I think it is for that reason that so many women demand open windows.

I hope Mr Mundy's wives see to it that his taste in tobacco is beyond suspicion!

(Mrs) I.M. Graham
Avening, Gloucestershire

SIR – The other day I had settled myself comfortably in a smoking carriage at Marylebone, and was reading when a party of men got in. One man immediately asked if anybody knew the subject for discussion that evening. Then the debate began, and they threw their remarks across the carriage as they might have done had they been still in the bar.

If instead of putting 'Smoking' or 'No smoking' on our railway carriages, we had 'Talking' or 'No talking', perhaps the women who wish to read could do so.

(Mrs) K.F. Rigg
Chorley Wood, Herts.

17 DECEMBER 1935

SIR – If your correspondent Mr Mundy were unfortunate enough to have to travel by the business trains leaving Manchester he would find almost every corner of every smoking compartment occupied by the gentler sex, from garrulous grandmothers to bawling babies.

On either side are compartments almost empty marked 'Smoking prohibited' or 'Ladies only'. Few of the ladies in them smoke, but they appear to be indignant if it is suggested that they might leave 'smokers' to men.

Any ordinary business concern would settle the matter in a few minutes.

C.H. Megson
Altrincham, Cheshire

18 DECEMBER 1935

SIR – I prefer to travel in a non-smoker and in an atmosphere in which I can enjoy my newspaper. One finds compartments labelled 'Ladies only', but none so marked for men.

If ' Ladies only' why not 'Gentlemen only'? There are thousands of us who would be glad to travel in the company of our fellows and be free from the gossiping of ladies.

Up men, and claim equality in at least one place where circumstances make it impossible to walk out!

Alec C. Sutherland
Barrow Road, SW16

19 DECEMBER 1935

SIR – You will, I know, be gratified to learn of yet another proof of your influence, following the correspondence on my letter of a few days ago about 'smoking' compartments on trains. Already my journey is vastly more agreeable.

The other evening the Christmas shoppers were huddled together in the 'non-smokers', exchanging optical hymns of hate. Both coming and going the next day I arrived warm and comfortable, full of Christmas spirit, and ready to enjoy the prosperity which we hear so much about.

It seems that antagonism to its own sex is not the only reason which impels woman to choose smoking carriages. One of the fair tells me that 'it is frightfully dull to travel in a carriage with a lot of women'. Another writes, anonymously but piteously, to suggest that lacking the means to wear expensive clothes she chooses a smoker because 'when a woman feels like half-a-crown, another woman looks at her and makes her feel fourpence'. Whereat I burst into tears.

I do not object to women in smoking carriages – only to those who lust for fresh air. This inordinate desire is as harmful as any other form of intemperance, and as anti-social. A temporary 'frowst' hurts no one – and is, moreover, productive of bonhomie and what-not.

Lionel Mundy
Great Castle Street, WI

23 DECEMBER 1935

SIR – May I contradict Mr Lionel Mundy? A 'temporary frowst' is highly objectionable to the large number of passengers who have no desire to breathe air just expelled from other people's lungs, however great their 'bonhomie and what-not'.

J.P.
Nunhead, SE15

27 JANUARY 1936
RAILWAY SIGNALLING

SIR — In the report of the inquest following the Shrivenham train accident it was stated that 'the guard dashed along the line with a lamp' to avoid a further crash.

Has not the time long since arrived for the railways to adopt a more effective method of warning in the event of a forcible stoppage?

In a letter of mine in *The Daily Telegraph* on July 2, in connection with the Welwyn disaster, I suggested that the railway companies should adopt a simple device such as a small searchlight. This could be fixed to the rear guard carriage of trains, so that in the event of a forcible stoppage it could readily be seen by the driver of an oncoming train.

I am now told that a ray has been invented which can be seen by day. This improved method of signalling would go a long way toward preventing accidents like the Welwyn and Shrivenham disasters.

B. Raperport
Hampstead

29 JANUARY 1936

SIR — One of your correspondents advocates a small searchlight for use at the rear of goods brake vans. There are grave objections to this, owing to the glare from the searchlight dazzling the driver of an oncoming train on an adjacent track.

The best and most inexpensive arrangement is a large enamelled sign in the form of a letter or cross mounted on the back of the van, which is visible from a distance in daylight and which can be electrically illuminated at night.

A.E. Williams
Deptford, SE14

1 JANUARY 1938

SIR – I enjoyed the friendship of a man who stood by George Stephenson when he started the 'Rocket' at Rainhill, on the Liverpool and Manchester Railway – the late Rev. E. L. Berthon, M.A., F.R.A.S., sometime vicar of Romsey, Hampshire. I joined the service of the old L. and S.W.R. in 1865, and I believe I was one of the very first men in the service of the company.

What your correspondents say about the dress of inspectors, 'The Crow's Nest,' &c., is correct. The passing of the guards' uniform I have always regretted. They wore frock-coats and patent leather cross-belts with silver-plated mountings. A watch was inserted in the suspended pouch.

Queen Victoria's guard wore a scarlet frock-coat. Telegraphists accompanied the Royal train, and there was a seat for the guard at either end of the carriage roof.

Trains in those days were sometimes roped in. I remember this being the case at Gosport, a station the like of which one does not see to-day. On nearing the station the driver stopped; the engine was switched on to the next rails; the draw rope was attached and the whole proceeded, the engine on one set of rails and the coaches on the other. By means of a second (slip) rope the guard would detach at the right moment.

The object was, presumably, to prevent the engine from smoking the station room. But I remember a case where the coaches failed to stop, and in their advance overthrew the massive stone-pillared iron gates.

J.J.H. (F.R.A.S.)
Honiton

10 OCTOBER 1939
MORE LIGHT IN THE TRAIN

SIR — The railway companies promise travellers better lighting in trains soon. But is there any sound reason why, on the electric services, something more nearly approaching normal lighting should not be restored?

The course of an electric train is at present obvious from the flashes from the conductor rail. The glow of lights would not tell a hostile airman any more than he knew already; and in any case the lights could be switched off as soon as the sirens were heard.

There seems to be even less point in the present gloom when one reads that, should a raid occur, underground trains will proceed after passengers who wish to leave have got out 'at the next station'.

Commuter
Richmond

12 NOVEMBER 1940

SIR – Should not the railways provide megaphones such as are used by boat race coaches and announcers at sports gatherings, on all stations, with a porter detailed to shout the name of the station during the hours of the black-out?

It is almost impossible for anyone making an unaccustomed journey to know what particular station is arrived at now that the names are all removed.

Clive Holland
Llandrindod Wells

30 SEPTEMBER 1941
TRAINS IN THE BLACK-OUT

SIR – Now that the black-out period is lengthening I would like to offer a suggestion. On railways two kinds of precautions are taken. One is that when the alert sounds all lights in trains are extinguished. That seems a wise and effectual precaution.

In addition to this, every day, and whether there is any air raid or not, all blinds are strictly drawn down, and even in the daylight hours the windows are surrounded with what may be called 'widows' mourning', and in some cases the side windows are blocked up altogether.

My suggestion is that the first precaution of extinguishing lights when a raid is signalled is effectual and sufficient, and that the other precautions of drawing down blinds and narrowing or blacking windows might wisely be discontinued.

It will be agreed that these precautions are extremely inconvenient. In what are called 'local' trains, where there are no corridors, and where the stop at a station is only for a minute, it is difficult to get into a train, since none can tell which carriages are already crowded, and without a corridor there is no way of passing from one carriage to another. Even at a station it is only the young and active that have time to descend from one carriage and find a better place in another. All this seems to cause superfluous suffering when all lights are extinguished as soon as the enemy approaches.

The extinction of lights is a more complete and effectual darkening than any blind-drawing; and before the raid begins what is the sense of blind-drawing? Why shut out light from an enemy who is not there?

I suppose that the precautions are mainly intended to preserve trains from attack and so protect civilian life. Civilian life is doubtless more important than civilian convenience, but it is not immeasurably more important. A great inconvenience should surely outweigh a slight and remote danger, and from the point of view of national morale I am sure that danger is a less serious menace than inconvenience.

Most people are like the lady in the 'Ingoldsby Legends' who 'did not mind death but she could not stand punching'. Small vexations are much more wearing to the will to victory than even grave dangers, and immensely more than slight ones. I urge, therefore, that we should retain the sensible precaution of darkening all trains when an air raid is signalled and give up the pulling down to blinds and putting our windows into 'widow's mourning'.

Lord Quickswood
The Lodge, Eton College

3 OCTOBER 1941

BLACK-OUT TRAVEL
Recapturing Lost Gift of Reflection

SIR — The darkness of railway carriages moves more passengers to write to the railways, and I expect to you, than any other single sacrifice we make to victory. In the main the letters to the railways are friendly letters written by people who know the difficulty and need for black-out and who do not suppose that the dim light is a symptom of dim management. But certainly it is a serious nuisance not to have enough light.

Once upon a time Charles Fox looked upon a journey in a coach as the best chance to compose a speech. The old labourer in *Punch*, when asked how he passed his time, would reply, 'Whiles I sits and thinks; whiles I just sits.' We have lost that habit of reflection, and when we are carried home tired at night we want to read the paper or at least to do the crossword.

Lord Quickswood in his letter to you suggested a radical cure — keep the full lights until the enemy approaches. This would solve the whole difficulty, but clearly A.R.P. and not the railways should decide. Much as I should like to agree with Lord Quickswood, I have no hope of his solution being adopted.

We must, I believe, continue to black-out windows and dim the lights of our railway carriages — much as we all dislike it — and the best comfort I can give my fellow sufferers is that the railways are fully conscious that their passengers want better light and are constantly seeking to improve.

Sir Alan Anderson
Ministry of War Transport, W1

30 JUNE 1944
OPEN THE WINDOWS

SIR — For five and a half years railway travellers have been advised 'in the event of an air raid to close all windows'. The idea was apparently protection against gas attack, though it was obvious that only carriages of most modern design could be made gasproof by closing the windows, and in them the ventilators cannot be closed.

It has been known for 100 years at least that when large guns were in practice the windows of neighbouring houses should be opened. Twice during air raids I have saved my windows by having windows and doors open.

Surely the order in the railway carriages should be reversed, and a general order issued to open all windows.

Prof. Morris W. Travers
Authors' Club, WC

5 JULY 1944
TRAVEL DE LUXE

SIR — The other evening one of our main-line trains, with every seat and every inch of standing room packed to capacity, drew up alongside a train carrying prisoners of war.

The Germans were eating and smoking in comfort — six to a first-class compartment and eight to a third-class compart - ment, with nobody standing, and the corridors empty except for an armed guard at either end. The rolling stock used was at least as modern as that on most main-line trains of to-day.

There is ample evidence that the public has no objection to its travel or comfort being curtailed in the interests of our own fighting men. But a great many people have vivid recollections of travel in the last war, for troops as well as prisoners, in wagons labelled '*Hommes 40 – Chevaux 8*'. And there are others who fail to see why exceptional comforts should be accorded even to the more fortunate of our bestial enemies.

Kenneth Edwards
Cmdr., RN
Naval and Military Club

10 JULY 1944

SIR – Cmdr. Kenneth Edwards's letter on his experiences when his crowded train passed one in which enemy prisoners were comfortably seated appears to show a lack of appreciation of the salient features regarding the two forms of travel [to] which he refers.

Many of our main-line trains are packed to capacity because the number of them has been reduced, while the numbers of travellers show practically no falling off whatever. For obvious reasons, standing in the corridors of the prisoners' train cannot be allowed. If it were permitted, attempts at escape would be invited.

Again, the rolling-stock of the prisoners' train might have been required at a certain point on the railway system the following day for a civilian train. Instead of working it empty between the two points, it was utilised for prisoners, thus effecting a considerable economy of available facilities. This is purely theoretical, but may quite likely have been the case.

Many factors, unknown to the public, may have combined to produce the circumstances deplored by Cmdr. Edwards.

G. Doyle Walker
West Byfleet

20 JULY 1944
CAPTIVE HERRENVOLK

SIR – Carefully verified reports of reliable eye-witnesses show that when the Germans occupied Poland and began to produce for themselves additional *Lebensraum* by expelling masses of Polish people from their homes in the western provinces, they transported men, women and children, the aged and the infirm, in locked and sealed cattle-trucks.

With deliberate cruelty they chose the winter season for these expulsions and hundreds of thousands were being kept for several days at a time permanently locked in freezing cattle-trucks, without food and without even the most elementary sanitary arrangements. Many thousands did not survive the journey.

I do not recommend a similar treatment for German prisoners of war reaching this country. But among them may be some who took part in these expulsions. Does it not stand to reason that they will be confirmed in their obsession of being a *Herrenvolk* if, after all they have done in the occupied countries, they are permitted such luxurious conditions of transport on the British railways as, apparently, the War Office has prescribed?

F.B. Czarnomski
Former London Correspondent of *The Courier of Warsaw*
London, NW3

14 NOVEMBER 1944
LUCKY FOREIGNERS

SIR – Travelling on the 4.28 train recently from London Bridge to Tunbridge Wells there were many Italian prisoners of war – four carriages were reserved for these men. The train was, as usual, crammed. Amongst the many who were standing in the corridors were some Tommies on leave, carrying their equipment. One of them exclaimed, 'Why are the Italians allowed reserved seats while we have to stand? Apparently it is better to be a foreigner in England nowadays.'

I can understand that these prisoners of war should be segregated, but are they? These men, who are in camp at Tonbridge, are allowed to wander at leisure throughout the town, so presumably segregation is not the reason for this high travel priority for these men, whom our soldiers have been fighting.

Incidentally, many women and small children were amongst those crammed in the corridors.

If the Government have any sound reason for giving travel priority to these Italians, why not publish it so that our soldiers and the public can understand? In the meantime much bitterness is being created and it is about time the responsible authorities did something about it.

E.R. Hill
London, EC

6 AUGUST 1945
BRIBERY?

SIR – If, when the railways are nationalised, one tips a porter will one be liable to a charge of corrupting a Government servant?

R.T.
Chelsea

22 JULY 1946
'YOUR RAILWAYS AMAZED ME!'
War Memories Of An American

SIR — If an American visitor may presume to voice an opinion, may I say I am amazed that Britain should even consider tampering with a phase of its national life in which it so excels — the management of its railroads?

American railroads performed miracles during the war. They put on a masterly show. But, to my view, the English surpassed it. Of this fact various illustrations spring to mind.

I spent some months here in those difficult days. Always I was startled by the comparative regularity of the services in and about London. Not because they were invariably on time — they were not — but because they were consistently so little late, V1s, V2s and the black-out notwithstanding.

Then there was the day I landed in England from North Africa — June 10, 1944, four days after D-Day. Our plane came down in Cornwall. Knowing what the confusion in Southern England must be, with millions of invasion troops packed into and squirming about in the tiny area, I estimated that our *Cornish Riviera Express* ought to get us into London five, eight or twelve hours late, at the least.

I was remembering what the large troop and supply movements had been doing to railway schedules in the Eastern Seaboard District at home. But, when the Great Western train rolled into Paddington that day we were 10 minutes ahead of time!

Britons contemplating nationalisation should think hard before raising the impairment of organisations which can do things like that.

Lee M. Schoen, London, NW1

24 JULY 1946

SIR — Mr Schoen's appreciation of the operation of our railways during the war, as seen through a visiting American's eyes, is opportune.

As a regular traveller between the City and Croydon I was rarely more than 10 minutes late at my office, in spite of the frequent warning 'Enemy Aircraft Overhead', and of explosions near enough to buffet the train. One must not forget also the depressing conditions during the winters of ice, snow and darkness outside, the dimly lit blacked-out carriages, and the courage of the depleted staffs, largely feminine. Has enough been said of those wonderful women who were always so cheerful?

A.C. Clark
Selsdon

1 NOVEMBER 1946
'SNEEZERS ONLY'

SIR — May I suggest that, as the season of coughs and sneezes that spread diseases approaches, the suburban trains should have a few compartments always marked and reserved for 'Sneezers Only'? If those qualified would share their miseries together they would give the rest a fighting chance of keeping fit.

J.T. Tripp
Forest Hill, SE

14 DECEMBER 1946

NATIONALISING IN THE DARK

SIR – The key sentence in your leading article on the Transport Bill is surely that in which you say that the public inquiry which the railway companies and road hauliers have called for, but the Government have refused, is 'as much needed to determine how to nationalise, as whether to nationalise'.

It would have been quite reasonable for the Government to have said, 'We are going to nationalise transport anyway, but we are perfectly willing to hold a public inquiry into the best means of achieving this.' If they had taken this course, we should not now be faced with a Bill which is, to say the least, quite impractical.

Let us take but one example. An inquiry would reveal that the railway companies, as at present grouped, are as large as can be efficiently managed. Such an inquiry would condemn on the grounds of operating inefficiency any proposal to combine the four groups into one. Yet that is the intention in the Bill. One railway executive will run all the railways – a colossal and impossible task, as any practising railway officer knows.

But having pledged themselves at the General Election to nationalise transport they prefer to take, as you say in your leader, 'a step in the dark on territory beset with all manner of pitfalls' rather than to accept the light of an inquiry which would illuminate the road they are taking.

Lt.-Cmdr. Lord Teynham
House of Lords

25 AUGUST 1947
TRAIN ANNOUNCERS

SIR — The introduction of oral announcements of train destinations is to be commended. One wonders, however, if sufficient discretion is used in selecting the announcers.

Efforts have been made to attract visitors from overseas, but it is doubtful if with an imperfect knowledge of our language they would find it easy to understand announcements at railway stations.

I am frequently reminded at a London station that trains are about to depart for — 'Orley, 'Orsham, 'Aywards 'Eath and 'Ove, and although it never fails to grate on the auditory nerve I can correctly interpret their destination. But would a foreigner be able to do so?

W. Figg
East Croydon

27 AUGUST 1947

SIR — The train announcements need reform which can be obtained by every company requiring announcers to get a certificate after a short training at an elocution school.

Other urgent reforms are: (1) No announcement during the noise of the train running in to the station. 2) All announcements should be slowly syllabic. It is the running of one syllable into the next which makes so many announcements unintelligible. (3) All announcements should be intoned. It is the experience of all Churches that intoning brings clarity in audition.

Josiah Oldfield, London, WI

SIR – As a native of Haywards Heath and a fairly frequent user of that section of the Southern Railway, I must differ from the recent statements made by Mr Figg.

On leaving Brighton a few weeks ago by a train stopping at the stations he mentioned, I particularly noticed the cultured tones of the women announcers.

J.P.R.T.B. Bacon Phillips (Rev.)
King's Lynn

29 NOVEMBER 1947
RAILWAY PRIDE

SIR – The Railway Executive Committee are to be applauded for dividing the British railways into six regions instead of the four as at present existing, for the L.N.E.R. and L.M.S.R. are in some ways too large for operating.

Is it too much to hope that the six regional chief officers will be allowed to exercise the functions of the present four general managers, and that each region will be allowed to design its own engines and rolling-stock and even paint them in their own distinctive colours?

Nationalisation need not mean complete standardisation, and there is much to be said for allowing pride in an individual region by such means as this, especially as a means of increasing efficiency.

W.K.A. Hussey
St John's College, Oxford

27 FEBRUARY 1948
REPAINTING THE TRAINS

SIR – There is a saying that 'If you have time to spare, travel by air,' and recent complaints would appear to afford some justification for what I regard as carping criticism. The air is not alone with delays.

By force of circumstances I was compelled last Friday to journey by rail to Newcastle, and thence to Edinburgh. I embarked on the *Flying Scotsman* at King's Cross and was immediately impressed by the punctuality of the start and the very modest speed at which we were translated over the countryside. In fact, the *Flying Scotsman* was the Crawling Scotsman.

We reached Peterborough, where, quite obviously, we changed engines. Breakdown No. 1. From then on we proceeded normally, reaching Newcastle an hour late.

The next day, full of hope. I took the 11.10 a.m. to Edinburgh. A handsome, modern, blue-painted and streamlined engine was attached to our train, and until Dunbar all went well. Just north of Dunbar we were shunted into a siding and an embarrassed member of the train crew told us the engine had broken down and we must wait for a new one from Dunbar or elsewhere. Breakdown No. 2. Finally, we reached Edinburgh two hours late.

Now, sir, Lord Inman is out to improve railway restaurants and hotels, and we, the public, are to be given the opportunity of pronouncing upon the colour we wish our nationalised locomotives painted. Would it not be better if the experts paid attention to locomotives, rolling stock and track maintenance, matters obviously of the first importance?

It is unfair to the public to draw publicity smoke-screens across the major deficiencies of our railways.

Before 1914, under private ownership, British railways

were good. After two periods — 1914–18 and 1939–45 — of Government control, they are a wreck. Two wars and all the political parties are to blame.

Is nationalisation going to put the railways on their feet, or will the extra cost of nationalised paint cause a disastrous stall and final crash?

Air Chief Marshal Sir P.B. Joubert
Sunningdale, Berks.

27 AUGUST 1948
FOOD ON WHEELS

SIR — I was interested to read of British Railways' experimental trolleys being used to take food to railway compartments over the heads of standing passengers.

It is encouraging to learn that corridors will continue to be used in the future by passengers who pay for seats.

Having on a recent occasion been unable to reach the dining-car owing to crowded corridors, may I suggest an even more novel technique for providing meals? The new scheme should be run in reverse, that is, passengers should be transported by conveyor from compartment to dining-car.

I trust this suggestion will provide British Railways and Lord Inman with plenty of food for thought.

J. Pearl
Hendon

14 APRIL 1950
GROWN-UP'S REBUKE

SIR – When will the Model Railway Club's exhibition be given its due, and cease to be referred to always as a children's paradise?

The exhibition is not designed for children, and I wonder that your reporter can be surprised at the greater number of adults attending. Nor are the exhibits toys – they are beautiful scale models, superb examples of craftsmanship.

As a railway modeller I know I shall enlist the support of all railway modellers in voicing this, our perennial, source of annoyance.

Peter A. Spring
Bramhall, Cheshire

20 JUNE 1950
GARISH TRAINS

SIR – Some weeks ago Lord Sempill protested in the House of Lords against the 'unlovely and impracticable' red and cream colour scheme of British Railways' coaches.

I have made some inquiries among my friends as to their reactions to the new livery. In no case has the reply been favourable, and all have been in essential agreement with Lord Sempill's description. 'Garish', 'gawdy', 'horrible', and 'reminiscent of a travelling circus' are some of the epithets used.

Some coaches freshly painted in the old Southern green have recently been noticed travelling northwards from Eastleigh. How much more suited to pass through the length and breadth of our green and pleasant countryside these seem than the glaring red vehicles now becoming standard.

Doubtless there are many conflicting views where colours are concerned. The 'lined out' black and the dark green liveries of locomotives, however, appear to be generally approved. Black would seem eminently suitable for a coal-consuming machine.

As to the insignia – Lord Sempill's 'uncomfortable lion' – the 'puir beastie' seems to be precariously balanced on a wheel, and is willy-nilly forced to proceed tail foremost when he decorates a tank engine running bunker first.

Frank E. Box
Winchester

23 JUNE 1950

SIR – Mr Frank E. Box must have been very unobservant a year or more ago.

At that time the Railway Executive took the trouble to run a series of trains in several different colour schemes over the whole country for many months.

Ample opportunity was given to members of the public to criticise these experimental colour schemes and public opinion was canvassed through the Press and on the radio. In these circumstances, criticism now is a little out of place and out of date.

Mr Box is evidently also unaware that green is the standard British Railways colour for all multiple unit electric stock, whether it is on the Southern or any other region.

Edward N. Soar
Worthing

SIR — Mr Box's criticisms of the livery of British Railways must reflect the opinion of many people.

Is it really necessary to nationalise the colour scheme? One of the simple pleasures of travel has been the sense of adventure aroused in, say, the Northerner who journeys from the workaday red or brown into the realm of chocolate and cream or unfamiliar green. Is it now quite out of the question for the various regions to retain some individuality as to colour?

As to the new badge, there is little to be said in its favour. It seems neither worthy nor very appropriate.

C.G. Wilson
Mexborough, Yorkshire

27 JUNE 1950

SIR — I think that those who are really interested in railway 'liveries' would like to see distinctive colour schemes for the different regions in place of the uninteresting uniformity which seems to be the present idea of British Railways.

Since some, at any rate, of the regions have already pleasing and familiar liveries these might surely have been retained as an economy as well as a concession to sentiment.

I am afraid Mr Frank Box's sight of freshly painted green stock for the Southern Region merely means that these coaches are to be used for electric traction. Steam-operated stock on this region is apparently being painted the red and cream which he and others deplore.

R.P. Hunwick
Barnet

29 JUNE 1950

SIR – Mr E.N. Soar's assumption as to my ignorance of the experimental trains and of the standard green for certain electric stock is neither correct nor to the point. What is relevant is that the vivid red now becoming standard for steam trains is regarded by many as unattractive and rather repellent.

Mr C.G. Wilson's point that we are losing much of the old-time pleasures of travel is sadly true, and many will agree with him that the retention by the regions of the old companies' liveries, each with their own territorial associations, would have been worth while. With what joy, for example, did the Sassenach, holiday-bound for Snowdonia, welcome the first glimpse of a Cambrian Railways' train in its distinctive white and sage green.

As a matter of history I recall seeing at Richmond in the late eighties, when the South Western sported the strange, but not unattractive, salmon and brown livery, a suburban train painted tentatively in dark green. Many years elapsed before that line eventually adopted green, which, after some changes of shade during the Southern regime, is now perpetuated in all British Railways multiple unit electric stock.

Perhaps, however, it is to Scotland that credit should be accorded for the first use of both the green and the crimson and white liveries, which were respectively those of the doughty old rivals, the Highland and Great North companies.

Frank E. Box
Winchester

SIR – Mr E.N. Soar is somewhat wide of the mark when he states that the Railway Executive ran experimental trains in different colour schemes 'over the whole country for many months' and that 'ample opportunity' was given for criticism.

In the south, for example, London–Chatham–Ramsgate and London–Bournemouth were the sole routes to see these trains, while in Wales the only train was one from London to Swansea. In fact, the only place where one could inspect the liveries to any advantage was London.

D.W. Winkworth
Tunbridge Wells

19 JANUARY 1951
PRIZES FOR TRAFFIC

SIR – When British Transport has to sink to such ridiculous, potentially barren and (to railwaymen) insulting schemes as 'prizes for traffic', then we seem to have reached the depths indeed. I hope your readers and the public generally will realise that this scheme has fermented in the brains of some of those in high places whose ideas are (to us on the railways) often weird and wonderful.

The plain fact is that the railways cannot efficiently deal with the traffic they now handle, let alone more of it. The main reason for this, as anyone carrying responsibility knows, is the deplorable staff situation. This is a reflection upon the Welfare State rather than the Railway Executive, but so long as men can earn more money and enjoy more regular hours and other conditions with private firms, often doing unskilled work, then the railway staff problem will get worse as the older stalwarts retire and die off. So will the railways.

As for nationalisation, I personally think that the greatest achievement has been the creation of a frustration hitherto unknown on the railways, in my 40 years' service.

Chief Parcels Clerk
London

24 MARCH 1951
'BAD OLD DAYS' WERE BETTER

SIR – From talks with railwaymen, I have been forced to the conclusion that nationalisation has not only failed to provide better and cheaper facilities for passengers and commerce, but brought no contentment to those engaged in the industry.

On a journey from London to the Midlands I spoke to the driver about the appearance of the engine, particularly the oil and grime he was wiping from the window of his cab. The driver informed me that he did not so much mind the poor turn-out of the engine, but that mechanically it was in a shocking condition. He showed me steam escaping from many joints, bolts with no nuts on them, and a number of other faults.

He had been 37 years on the railway, he added, and had always enjoyed his work, but recently things had been becoming almost unbearable. Day after day he filled in a repairs card, but nothing was done, and the attitude of the fitters and others in the shed was unhelpful. 'If this is what Socialism and nationalisation does,' he concluded, 'give me the bad old days.'

J. McDermid
Edenbridge

4 SEPTEMBER 1951
OIL-DRIVEN TRAINS

SIR — Peterborough's note on the Western Region gas-turbine locomotive brings to mind the need for up-to-date traction on the railways. Out of a stock of some 20,000 locomotives held by British Railways at the end of last year, there were under 200 diesel electric or diesel railcars on the whole system. In America, over 40 per cent of the traffic is hauled by diesel or diesel electric motors, and 98 per cent of the orders placed for locomotives require diesel operation. In fact, large-scale manufacture of steam locomotives has long been abandoned in the United States. European countries, too, are well ahead of this country in this modern trend.

If we want to save coal and to get a much higher use out of our engines, then we have every incentive to change from coal to oil. Using oil on the railways and releasing coal for export to countries where it will buy so much would actually show a foreign exchange profit.

R. Gresham Cooke
Director, Society of Motor Manufacturers and Traders
London, WI

22 FEBRUARY 1952
FUNERAL ENGINE

SIR — Many will have read with mixed feelings about the deception practised by British Railways about the engine pulling the Royal funeral train. Some will have wondered whether the old Great Western Railway would have been guilty of such cynicism.

But having committed themselves, why did the authorities change the name-plates back again afterwards? There are precedents for transferring a famous old name to a new holder – the famous old liner *Mauretania* and the present *Mauretania*, for example.

Why should not the *Bristol Castle* be permanently renamed the *Windsor Castle*, so that everyone in future will know it was the engine which pulled the funeral train? The original *Windsor Castle* is so old that it will not need a name-plate much longer.

John Littlejohns
Lee, SE

SIR – I am shocked by the disclosure that the engine which drew the late King to Windsor was the *Bristol Castle* masquerading as her elder sister the *Windsor Castle*, not only in name and number, but even wearing the plate commemorating that George V had driven her.

That *Windsor Castle* should chance to be out of service was unfortunate, but how could a deception be thought more fitting than the use of *Bristol Castle* under her own name?

This pointless impersonation, whether it be regarded as mere childishness or a pathetic error of judgement, is made all the worse by the memory of the late King's interest in engineering and his supreme sense of honour.

Geoffrey Parks
Battle

A number of other letters to the same effect have been received.

16 SEPTEMBER 1952
RAILWAY MEALS

SIR – I have recently taken two railway journeys involving a number of meals, one to Scotland and one to Cornwall. The food on the journey to Scotland was deplorable, but on the Cornish one quite good and nearly worth the charge. The variation in the quality, cooking and choice of food was most marked.

Why, when British Railways own the whole system? I hope the travelling public will protest against the high charge for inferior meals. The biscuits served with early morning tea are of the cheapest quality, and who wants a sweet biscuit at 7.30 a.m.?

The Railway Executive have now decided on Holland linen (I call it sacking) to serve as mats in the sleeping compartments. If mats are now considered essential, why not have mats and not totally unsuitable material which gives quite pleasant sleeping compartments the appearance of convicts' cells?

Miss Irene Ward, M.P.
House of Commons

18 SEPTEMBER 1952

SIR – In her letter about railway meals and additional mats in sleeping compartments, Miss Irene Ward, M.P., does not mention that she recently put her complaints to the Chairman of the British Transport Commission, who has given her a complete answer. After careful enquiry we do not accept her description of the meals she took on trains in Scotland.

As regards the linen mats, we have told Miss Ward that these have been provided, on top of the carpeting on the West Coast route for some time, and because they are appreciated by many passengers, they are now available in sleeping cars via the East Coast.

J.H. Brebner
British Transport Commission
London, SW

20 DECEMBER 1952

SIR – Some months ago the British Transport Commission Public Relations Officer stated he did not accept my views on various matters relating to a train journey to Scotland. In particular my complaint about baked haddock was dismissed on the ground that haddock was never served on British Railways. I therefore appealed to the Transport Users' Consultative Committee.

After re-examination of my complaint I have received an abject apology from the Hotels Executive with the explanation that there was a flaw in the administrative machine. Apparently they were unaware that restaurant cars in Scotland have a separate control from England, and the inquiry on my meals complaint could never have been examined at all, but a general reply without investigation sent me. So much for writing to the Chairman of the British Transport Commission.

As I have received no apology from either Lord Hurcomb or Mr Brebner, I can only assume that they have not been informed of the fact that they were wrongly advised to challenge my haddock statement.

I wonder how often the criticisms of the general public are dismissed through similar flaws in the channels of communication.

Miss Irene Ward, M.P.
House of Commons

30 DECEMBER 1952

SIR – Miss Irene Ward, M.P., writes to complain to you about baked haddock being served on British Railways.

But if Miss Ward ever has to travel to her constituency from London on the 4.45 express on a Sunday afternoon she will not be served with baked haddock or with any other British Railways delicacy. For, although this express is well patronised, so little do British Railways care for the comfort of the travelling public that they do not provide on it either a restaurant car or even a buffet car, and few, if any, platform trolleys are provided at the stops en route.

I am told that there have been hundreds of complaints by the public, but when I took the matter up with the Chairman of the Railway Executive in October, I was merely informed, 'The possibility of running a car has been constantly in mind. Unfortunately there is no satisfactory balancing service with this train.'

So far as I know, the matter is still in mind. For, in spite of several reminders, I have still to hear that a 'balancing service', whether of baked haddock or otherwise, has yet been found by British Railways.

In the meantime I strongly advise Miss Ward and other travellers to the North to avoid this train. Unfortunately it seems to be a train which is much patronised by foreign visitors and their comments on the lack of facilities are only equalled by their amazement.

Mr Rupert M. Speir, M.P.
House of Commons

21 DECEMBER 1953
HAPPY GESTURE

SIR – At one time it was quite usual for passengers arriving at any railway terminus, after a long-distance run, to pass a word of thanks to the engine driver and his fireman who had brought them safely to their destination.

Such a gesture is seldom made to-day and more the pity. Now that the threat of a major railway strike has been averted what better opportunity, at this season of goodwill, for the public to show their appreciation to, at least, some of the men who have made their rail travel possible.

D. Knight
Aldershot

5 FEBRUARY 1954
CHILLY TRAINS

SIR – It would be interesting to know whether our railway authorities are satisfied with the design of present equipment for heating trains.

It is understandable that water systems should freeze up when coaches necessarily stand at sidings for long periods in cold weather. What is less understandable is why, when heat in coaches is really needed during a journey, it is all too often dissipated or held up by a stoppage in the system.

Forty years ago Russian trains were well heated; if they still are perhaps the Russian heating system is worth our study. What are our railway authorities doing about the problem anyway?

Air Vice-Marshal F.H.M. Maynard
Colyford, Devon

8 FEBRUARY 1954
USEFUL SAMOVAR

SIR – I travelled by the Trans-Siberian Railway from Manchouli to Moscow in 1935. The heating in my carriage was efficient, but I noted with interest that it had been built in England in 1915. At the same time I should say that the only facilities for hot water were provided by a samovar at the end of the corridor.

Brig. A.F. Stokes-Roberts
London, SW15

9 FEBRUARY 1954
RUSSIAN TRAVEL

SIR – Air Vice-Marshal Maynard's comparison between chilly trains in Britain and the warmth of those in Russia 40 years ago reminds me of my own experience in more recent times.

Travelling 'soft' – I believe that was the official designation of our class – I found with surprise that the first thing to be dealt with in our compartment was to release the windows which had been nailed (yes, nailed) shut. This was achieved by the ingenious use of penknives and pliers, and created a certain amount of consternation, but no actual opposition, from the station officials.

Doubtless this enforced lack of ventilation contributed materially to the warmth of the travellers within.

Secondly, the snail-like progress of the train – it was on the main line from Moscow to Odessa – undoubtedly per-mitted a greater proportion of the steam to be diverted from the boiler for heating purposes than could be permitted here.

Finally, the frequent and extended stops at every station

allowed one to alight for refreshment. Afterwards it was possible to take invigorating exercise by walking up and down the length of the train several times.

Certainly, though a little tedious, Russian travel was not without its benefits. It was at least warm and safe, and we got there in the end.

Harold Cadoux
Rugby

22 MAY 1954
UNOFFICIAL STRIKES

SIR — What has happened to the locomotive engineers and firemen on the Western section of British Railways? The drivers and stokers of the old Great Western Railway were once among the most loyal supporters of their union, with a very high sense of duty to their railway and to the public.

Now they are indulging in an unofficial strike because, as I understand, they are asked to spend one night in 10 away from their homes and families.

I wonder whether they have thought what would happen to their tea or their tobacco (and many other things) if seamen of the merchant navy took a similar view.

We have just celebrated the safe return of our Queen and her husband, who have been separated on duty by many hundreds of miles from their home for six months and from their young children for nearly as long.

Earl Stanhope
Sevenoaks

4 JUNE 1954

AFTER THE STRIKE

SIR – I live at Newton Abbot and many of my friends are railwaymen; therefore I am certainly not prejudiced against them. On the contrary I am much concerned at the harm done to them by recent events – and I know that many of them think the same.

I also have my lodging turn problems because I am a commercial traveller – away four or five nights every week for the last 30 years, and throughout most of that period a fare-paying passenger on the railways (without the benefit of free holiday travel).

The firm which I represent has been loyal to the railways for 80 years, and in that time must have paid the railways a huge sum of cash for transport charges. But last week the firm switched over to road vehicles as thousands of others probably did. It may not be easy for the railways to regain that lost business.

The strike is now presumably over. Already the cry of 'No victimisation' has been raised. Is that not adding insult to injury?

The very essence of every strike is victimisation, immediate and continued, of every ordinary member of the community, and let us face it, never has any strike flared up on more flimsy pretext than this one.

I plead not only for a sense of responsibility (meaning 'duty') but for a sense of proportion as well. 'No victimi - sation' if properly interpreted should mean 'No more strikes'.

H.W. Harding
Bath

6 MAY 1955
ECHO OF THE TORS

SIR — Most Devonians, I am sure, will be grieved to hear of the proposed closing of the Princetown branch railway. Not only is it an essential link between the moorland town and the outside world, but it provides a series of excellent starting-points for the moor-walker.

Burrator Halt serves the Lake and the Sheepstor region and the Halt at Ingra Tor was built as recently as 1936 by the old Great Western Railway for this specific purpose. King Tor Halt, three miles farther on, has served as a good base for reaching Great Mis Tor and the upper valley of the Walkham.

Princetown station itself handles most of the passengers who seek escape to Plymouth from their depressing surroundings, while offering to the visitor an approach to Two Bridges, Wistman's Wood and the Nun's Cross area. Among the freight is a considerable traffic in ponies at the time of the autumn sales.

It will be a sorry thing, sir, if the tors no longer echo to the voice of the valiant little 2-6-2 tank engine as it struggles to lift its one or two coaches up the 900ft climb from Yelverton. As a scenic route and an example of engineering in the face of extreme difficulties the line deserves preservation for its own sake.

T.W.E. Roche
Dover

2 JANUARY 1957
TRAVELLERS' TRIALS

SIR – Heartened by the news before Christmas that a billiards table had made the cross-country journey by rail from Salford to Stroud in record time, we thought it would be a simple matter to travel from London to North Wales. This, alas! was not the case.

Some of our party (four adults and two children) entrusted themselves on Dec. 21 to the 5.30 p.m. from Euston to Bangor. It was due to arrive at 10.20 p.m., but did not reach its destination until after 2 a.m.

Slight fog earlier in the day may partly have accounted for the delay, but nothing had been omitted which could contribute to the passengers' acute discomfort. There was no food or drink on the train, the restaurant car having been forgotten. Not once during all those hours did a guard walk along the corridors.

In our friend's compartment neither the window nor the door into the passage could be persuaded to close, and it was necessary to sit in a permanent draught, the inadequate heating not trickling through for several hours.

We, who took the night mail to Holyhead that same evening, fared slightly better. After spending two hours on the platform we were able to crawl into our icy cabins. That was not the luck of the unfortunates who had booked second-class sleepers – only to find their coach had not been attached.

The Christmas rush always seems to come as a complete surprise to British Railways. Would it not be kinder if they issued a warning: 'To those intending to travel: Don't'?

Lady Juliet Duff
Wilton, Wiltshire

14 MARCH 1957
MIXTURE AS BEFORE

SIR — As a 'locomotophile' (if that be the term for somebody who has a 55-year-old affection for railways), I take a particular pleasure in eating in restaurant cars — supposing, that is, that the eatables provided are even remotely eatable.

The other day I travelled to Manchester on the 11.45 a.m. from Euston. The fare British Railways offered (at 8s 6d per head) consisted of lentil soup, fried plaice or roast beef and Yorkshire pudding, Manchester pudding or ice-cream and fruit salad or cheese and biscuits.

From this galaxy of attractions I chose the soup, the beef, the ice-cream. It was not a classic meal, but it served to pass the time.

On the following day I travelled back to London on the 9.55 a.m. and in the restaurant car found myself faced with precisely the same menu, except that the fairly succulent green peas had been replaced by the largest and wettest brussels sprouts ever dug out of a 'deep freeze'.

Surely something can be done not so much to improve the railway menu (which needs it, heaven knows) as to vary it.

Eric Maschwitz
London, WI

18 MARCH 1957
MONOTONOUS TEAS

SIR — May I support Mr Eric Maschwitz on railway meals, particularly with reference to the unchanging monotony of train teas?

Wherever one travels on the British Railways system, the

composition of teas never varies — toasted teacake, slices of buttered bread, jam, and some sort of cake or biscuits.

J.S. Dinwiddie
Dumfries

20 MARCH 1957
CRUMPETS EN ROUTE

SIR — I was surprised to read Mr J.S. Dinwiddie's allegation of the unchanging monotony of the teas served on trains and would be glad to have any suggestion he cares to make.

I quote a typical meal for afternoon tea on restaurant cars:

Tea, Indian or China

Toast or toasted teacake

A choice of preserves of at least four varieties

Bread and butter, a choice of brown or white

Fruit or plain cake, or pastries or chocolate biscuits.

In addition, on certain trains where the demand is known to be present, we serve crumpets. We have experimented with a service of Devonshire cream teas on some trains, but this met with a poor response.

The cost of 2s 6d, which we consider to be very reasonable, places a certain limit on what can be served, but the menu does compare favourably with that of any other catering organisation.

Your correspondent may be interested to know that more than 6m. teas were served on trains last year.

J.H. Brebner
Transport Commission, NW1

SIR – I could not sympathise more with Mr. J.S. Dinwiddie in his despair about dull British Railways teas.

It is bad enough to be helplessly exposed to dining-car cooking (roasted boilers, ubiquitous cabbage, neutral-tasting ice-cream and astonishing coffee), but it is a shame that tea, a most enjoyable British meal, is turned into a stodgy deterrent.

Why cannot we have:

Feather-light scones, made a few hours before the train leaves;

Buttered toast, toasted and served only a few slices at a time, so that they stay really hot;

Small, appetising, savoury-sandwiches, filled with liver-paté, cream cheese, chopped eggs, &c. (even canapés would be inexpensive and a question of organisation);

Fruit cakes in taste, not only in appearance; very much lighter sponge cakes and tartlets; and a glimmer of variety (for example, maids of honour or fresh fruit tartlets, to mention a few)?

It cannot be done at the present set charge of 2s 6d? Then either the price should be increased or the items charged separately.

Will British Railways ever follow the example of recently improved catering standards in restaurants? Or is this renaissance to founder on bureaucratic complacency?

Egon Ronay

23 MARCH 1957

SIR – When they criticise the teas served on trains, what do Mr J.S. Dinwiddie and Mr Egon Ronay except for 2s 6d? After all, it is only afternoon tea, not a slap-up meal.

Considering the increase in charges of all goods and services since 1939 and the declining value of the pound, it is remarkable that the British Railways' charge for tea is not 4s.

Mr Ronay's suggestion that there should be various savoury sandwiches is not a good one. I should say the majority of travellers do not want this sort of stuff at tea-time. What, by the way, are canapés? Let us be British and stick to the good old tea, toast and jam.

W. Naylor Turner
Sunderland

26 MARCH 1957
WINKLES FOR TEA

SIR – Among the many helpful suggestions put forward for improving the catering on British Railways one has been overlooked.

May I propose that, beside crumpets, canapés, cakes and other farinaceous concoctions, there should be included the time-honoured shrimps and winkles?

H.M. Bateman
North Tawton, Devon

7 AUGUST 1957
BAGGAGE SMASHERS

SIR – Damage to trunks while in transit by rail or road is not confined to this country. Railway porters in the United States are not known as 'baggage smashers' because of the gentleness with which they handle passengers' luggage.

From personal observations it would seem that too many

porters and vanmen are just 'too tired' to put an article down. They have to throw or drop it.

However, as in other spheres, a service is taken for granted as long as it is good, while it is only the faults that seem to be publicised.

B. Murton
Plymouth

SIR – I do not think you are quite fair to British Railways or their employees. At 12 o'clock one recent Friday night I saw some happy railway porters folk-dancing on No. 2 platform at Basingstoke.

One would not have seen this before nationalisation.

John Minter Phillips
Southampton

7 OCTOBER 1957
ELEVENSES

SIR – Recently I arrived at King's Cross in good time to catch the 10.30 a.m. train to Hertford. A courteous taxi driver helped me unload my luggage and I went in quest of a porter, but was unable to find one.

Eventually I discovered five porters drinking tea in the buffet. With one accord they refused to take my luggage, as none had finished his tea. I missed my train and was forced to wait one hour for the next.

Does the railway porter come under the category of civil servant? If so, whose servant is he, and to whom is he civil? One cannot help but wonder.

Anthony Heckstall-Smith
Hertford

7 DECEMBER 1957
TRAIN CONTROL

SIR – In this age of science, where electronics play a prominent part, it seems ridiculous that a railway warning system has not been universally developed to work effectively in foggy conditions.

British Railways should ensure the safety of all who use their somewhat ageing facilities.

R.E. Hardy
Kenilworth, Warwickshire

10 DECEMBER 1957

SIR – Mr R.E. Hardy seems to me to do less than justice to British Railways. The Western Region has inherited a system of automatic train control that has proved its reliability in all weathers for 50 years.

Twice only in this period – at Norton Fitzwarren in 1940, and at Milton in 1955 – has an accident occurred which this safety device should have prevented. In each case the failure lay with the human element, which electronics can never totally replace.

During the last 10 years this device has been under constant study and experiment in the hands of railway engineers, who have had to face serious technical problems in adapting it for general use with electric traction.

That the work of equipping our main lines with so valuable a safety device is already in progress is surely another tribute to scientific achievement rather than a symptom of what your correspondent describes as the 'ageing facilities' of British Railways.

(Rev.) E.M. Geoghegan
Downside Abbey, Bath

5 JANUARY 1958
FROM THE MACHINE

SIR – Your report about the lack of nocturnal amenities at the London railway termini showed that, in this as in other respects, they compare unfavourably with many of their Continental counterparts.

The answer to the objection of the Transport Commission that the supply of hot meals would be uneconomic from the staffing point of view was given, however, on Page 11 of the same issue of *The Daily Telegraph*.

In 'Around American To-day' appeared the following: 'American slot machines, which provide a range of articles from cigarettes to hot coffee, made more than £700m. in sales last year, a record. Manufacturers are trying to design a fully cooked meal in 20 seconds.'

British Railways could, therefore, at least make a start with hot drinks, to be followed, when machines are available, by *Tripe à la mode de Charing Cross* and *Crêpe Fenchurch Street*.

Gerald Sullivan
Luebeck, Germany

23 MAY 1958
RAILWAY KINDNESS

SIR — Several correspondents have written concerning the misdeeds and shortcomings of British Railways. May I say something on the other side?

As vicar of a parish it is frequently my duty to arrange excursions for parties, mostly for children. Such parties have always met with the most friendly co-operation from the railway authorities and the staffs at all the stations concerned. And when I say 'always' I mean just that.

Another instance. I was once returning from the continent, with some young Dutch people travelling with me. One of them was a vegetarian. I went to the dining-car and interviewed the head steward, and he came to the compartment and discussed the matter with the young lady concerned. She was supplied with a very satisfactory meal fulfilling all her requirements and actually costing less than the more usual dinner.

Recently, at a very busy time, a relative of mine left her handbag on a seat at a busy station. Realising this, she spoke to the guard, who telephoned back from the next stop. One station farther on news was brought that the handbag had been found and would be returned to the owner in two days. It was so returned, with its contents intact, including an appreciable sum of money. The charge for this service was less than 3s.

George F. Naylor
London, SW19

23 FEBRUARY 1959

SIR – I have been astounded during my three years' residence in this country at the appalling loss of life, limb and money on each occasion the railway system is affected by fog.

Monotonously each disaster seems to be caused by the signalling system. Is this really such a big problem as it is made out to be? I know from personal experience of an extensive and congested suburban system on the other side of the world which on occasions is affected by dense fog.

The electro-mechanical signalling system prevents a driver taking his electric train or steam locomotive past a signal set against him. To proceed he has first to descend from his cab to the track to re-set the brake trip, which had been actuated automatically from beside the track in unison with the semaphore arm and lights of the signal.

I believe all this equipment was made in England or under licence in Australia. There has not been a serious accident by collision for 35 years or more in Melbourne, and seldom is there a delay of more than a couple of minutes by trains on this system, whose motto is 'On time all the time'.

H.G. Woollam
Fetcham, Surrey

26 FEBRUARY 1959
RAIL SAFETY

SIR – The sweeping statements made by Mr H.G. Woollam that there is an 'appalling loss of life, limb and money on each occasion when the railway system is affected by fog', and that 'each disaster seems to be caused by the signalling system', are unsupported by a shred of evidence.

The signalling system on British Railways is as good as elsewhere in the world, and enables them to deal with a high density of traffic, traditionally the highest in the world, in an incomparably safer manner than any other form of transport.

The signalling device to which Mr Woollam refers is well known to British Railways and is similar to that which has been in use on London Transport railways for many years.

It has been found unsuitable, however, for main lines, where automatic train control, providing visual and audible warnings of a signal at caution, followed by an automatic application of the brake if these are ignored, is considered the best kind of aid to the train driver. This system is in use on 1,356 route miles of the former G.W.R., on 188 route miles between London (King's Cross) and York, on 47 route miles of the London (Fenchurch Street) to Southend lines, and is being rapidly extended on four other main routes.

We are not ashamed of our record of safety on British Railways, but there is no complacency and we are neglecting no available resource of expenditure or effort to make it even better.

J.H. Brebner
Public Relations Adviser, British Transport Commission
London, NW1

4 MARCH 1959

SIR – I must thank Mr J.H. Brebner for his reply to my letter in your columns.

I stated that 'each railway disaster seems to be caused by the signalling system'. Mr Brebner contends that this statement cannot be 'supported by a shred of evidence'. Without going into detail I would say that the Lewisham smash in itself is more than 'a shred of evidence'. If the signalling method I mentioned had been installed it would have been impossible for the train responsible for the disaster to have passed the signal set against it.

Mr Brebner further supports my argument by mentioning sections of the British Railways system that are equipped with a fully protected signalling system, the largest of which, the former G.W.R., accounts for a meagre 1,356 route miles. This is not a newfangled system. Why cannot the Southern and other regions be similarly protected as a national emergency *now* before there is an even greater loss of life, limb and money?

H.G. Woollam
Fetcham, Surrey

2 JUNE 1959

SOMBRE BRITISH SERVICE

SIR – Having travelled a great deal on the Continent, I cannot be unimpressed by the service, civility and attention shown by waiters and restaurant-car attendants.

When I returned recently from the Continent and boarded the train at Folkestone, it took exactly one hour for the sombre dining-car attendant to serve four trays of tea. To cap it all, a frigid-looking girl came round with ices who said: 'Do you want any ices?' with a voice as frigid as the products she was trying to sell.

One wonders what Continental visitors must think of Britain and the service given. I am British, and proud of it, but the above is no advertisement. Incidentally, the train was as frigid as the attendants.

A.A.V. Haddy
London, NW7

16 JUNE 1959
RAILWAY'S FRIENDLY WAITER

SIR – Having read Mr A.A.V. Haddy's letter concerning the poor service in the restaurant cars of British Railways, I feel that I must come to the defence of some of the waiters.

Last autumn I travelled from St Pancras to Sheffield and had dinner *en route*. I refused the meat course and asked for vegetables only. The waiter was most concerned and asked if he could find something I would like better.

With a very solemn face he said: 'I'll ask the engine driver to put his rod and line out over the next river and see whether he can catch you some fish,' removed my plate and, 10 minutes later, returned with beautifully grilled fillets of plaice and a fresh supply of vegetables.

I had delayed the service, as I was taking the 'first' sitting. I was travelling second class and I am certainly no glamour girl but a middle-aged lady who was accompanied by a husband and son.

M.M. Chapman
Sheffield

31 JULY 1959
DEATH BY RAILWAY LUNCH

SIR – Peter Simple's story of the rhinoceros that expired after eating the contents of a British Railways packed lunch has caused considerable concern to British Transport Catering Services and their suppliers.

His anecdotes are well appreciated by a wide public, but by describing deliberately the packed lunch as one prepared by British Transport he is quite unfair to them and their suppliers.

In my experience they buy high-quality products from firms of national repute, and this fact would be well known to any users of railway station catering facilities.

R.E. Doubleday
Managing Director, R.E. Doubleday & Co. Ltd.
London, SW2

3 AUGUST 1959
A RHINO'S DEATH

SIR – Mr R.E. Doubleday's concern about Peter Simple's story of the rhinoceros that expired after eating a British Railways packed lunch is appreciated. I assume from this letter that his firm's products were not to blame.

He is apparently acting as spokesman for the British Transport Commission's catering services, for he states that the story has caused concern in official circles. It is surprising that an official statement has not been issued on the subject, for the B.T.C. usually defends its services with the utmost vigour.

Let there be a public inquiry on this subject which Mr Doubleday takes so seriously. I would suggest Peter Simple as its chairman. The Royal College of Veterinary Surgeons should be asked for an autopsy, and Mr Doubleday should be called on to watch the interests of rhinos who rely on British Railways catering facilities.

But where is the dead rhino? Lying in the lost property department of a station on a closed branch line?

H. Leech
London, EC3

SIR – Peter Simple states that the rhino died after eating a British Railways packed lunch. Mr R.E. Doubleday stoutly denies that such a packed lunch of quality products can be lethal, and resents such a deliberate implication.

Dr Watson, with whom I have some slight acquaintance, writes in his very old age to say that he feels sure that Holmes would have thought all the evidence pointed to the fact that cardboard boxes could not be consumed with safety. Dr Watson adds that in other respects he is certain that the cardboard box fills its purpose admirably, and with such good wishes all round he hopes that honour is satisfied.

E.B. Robinson
Managing Director, Robinson & Sons, Ltd.
Chesterfield, Derbyshire

6 AUGUST 1959

SIR – I see from Mr E.B. Robinson's letter that, with the aid of an aged member of the medical profession, he blames the indigestibility of the cardboard box as the cause of the unfortunate demise of Peter Simple's rhinoceros.

Surely this incident is a challenge to Mr Robinson's firm. Could it not manufacture a digestible cardboard box, if necessary in different flavours (strawberry, vanilla, mild and bitter)?

Not only would this help any rhino who is in the habit of eating packed lunches. It would also be one way out of the litter problem.

John Furniss
Ashford, Middlesex

SIR – Mr R.E. Doubleday has got a lot, I see, to say on rhinos who sit down and munch a British Railways pre-packed lunch.

I for my part would like to see a lead from the judiciary protecting the œsophagus of every stray rhinoceros. The railways, on the other hand, could take a somewhat firmer stand and reject food from any firm which might upset a pachyderm.

Ian Ferguson
Sellindge, Kent

3 AUGUST 1959
MAIN LINES

SIR – In the latest published plans for improving the railways by gradually doing away with them there is one particularly ominous statement, viz., that 'no closure of main lines between now and 1965 is foreseen at present'. So the rot is well set in, and the Transport Commission can give no guarantee if and when this process can cease.

Not many years ago few would have believed that such integral sections of our railway system as the Midland and Great Northern line in East Anglia, and the Crystal Palace High Level suburban line, and many others, would soon be little more than a memory. However, judged by present trends, one can well visualise many main-line termini, and possibly the newly electrified Kent Coast line, as derelict sites within 10 years or so.

John C.H. Nunn
Sevenoaks, Kent

16 SEPTEMBER 1959
RUSSIAN ROCKET

SIR — If the Russians can manage to send a rocket to the moon within two minutes of the scheduled time, when may we expect British Railways to emulate this magnificent achievement and run their trains to the advertised time of arrival?

Grenville Collins
London, SW1

25 SEPTEMBER 1959
ON TIME

SIR — Mr Grenville Collins wonders when the thousands of trains operated daily by British Rail will achieve the punctuality of a solitary Russian rocket establishing contact with a lunar surface roughly the size of North America. (Arrival in the middle of a lunar Lake Superior instead of at a lunar Salt Lake City is apparently of little consequence provided journey's end can be accurately described as lunar.)

Perhaps Mr Collins has never had the good fortune to witness the entry into Brighton terminus, not of the Queen of Sheba, but of the more impressive *Brighton Belle*.

A surprise of porters (I hope that is the correct collective noun) assembled on a central platform separates into widely spaced groups as, far out in the daylight beyond the confines of the station, a small brown object appears which gradually increases in size until it enters the twilight under the great roof. Then comes the difficult feat of keeping one eye on the clock and the other on the dark brown and cream and the lampshades of slowly moving Pullman cars.

Twenty seconds to go; ten; 5-4-3-2 — a barely perceptible

67

jerk denotes the cessation of the train's motion as the minute hand of the clock stands dead on the hour. Even the ranks of Tuscany, casually filing out on to the platform after a discreet pause, look a little pleased, as if they had had something to do with the performance.

L.B. Nulty
Hayward's Heath, Sussex

13 OCTOBER 1959
BRIGHTON BELLE IS OUTCLASSED

SIR – Mr L.B. Nulty's proud letter about the time-keeping of the *Brighton Belle* Pullman train seems to me an example of a British tendency to judge British things by a British, rather than a world, yardstick.

The *Brighton Belle* averages only 55 m.p.h. over a journey of, of course, 55 miles. This makes the train about the slowest and shortest 'named' run in Europe. Even the Bristolian manages only 72 m.p.h. over 100 miles, and on runs of 300 miles and upwards Britain's best is not above 65 m.p.h. On these runs punctuality is, as your earlier correspondent inferred, all over the place.

The real yardstick of speed and punctuality that we should all (including British Railways) have in mind is the Mistral, which covers the 317 miles from Paris to Lyons at an average of 77 m.p.h. The Mistral is late about as often as Big Ben.

Correlli Barnett
Weybridge, Surrey

14 OCTOBER 1959

SIR – *The Brighton Belle* train is even slower than Mr Correlli

Barnett thinks. The distance from Victoria to Brighton is only 50¾ miles, not 55.

E.A. Gurney-Smith
Sevenoaks, Kent

15 OCTOBER 1959

SIR — In describing my reference to the punctuality of the *Brighton Belle* as 'an example of a British tendency to judge British things by a British, rather than a world, yardstick', Mr Correlli Barnett appears to be unaware that I wrote with a certain amount of what I hoped would be regarded as British humour, in reply to another British humorist, Mr Grenville Collins, who wanted to know when British railway trains could be expected to emulate a Russian moon rocket and arrive 'on time'.

In any case, after the ordeal of travelling at 93 m.p.h. in a pre-war Atlantic Coast Express which left Salisbury 40 minutes late and arrived at Waterloo, unlike the itinerant Grouchy, dead on time, I strongly advise regular patrons of the *Brighton Belle* on no account to strike for a 35-minute run. Really high speeds have to be experienced to be believed.

Mr Barnett quotes the 78 m.p.h. Mistral as an example of railway efficiency, but surely the only criterion in the case of important express trains is what happens to a plate of soup ordered en route. Is it brought *in toto* and consumed in comfort, or does the arrival of an empty plate suggesting low tide at Southend signify that the *Ci-devant* contents have gone with the Mistral? That is the question.

L.B. Nulty
Hayward's Heath, Sussex

SIR — A comparison of French train speeds with British is unhelpful because of the very different operating conditions. In this country we have some of the densest traffic in the world, and this makes it difficult to find a 'path' for a very high speed train. In France conditions are not so exacting, and we must not forget that although the speeds attained by such trains as the Sud Express and the Mistral are in many ways admirable, the fares charged are rather less so.

What do we find in Britain? Trains in all regions reach 100 m.p.h. in places every day, and no supplement is exacted. Let us take the Bristolian for instance. Even in the days of steam haulage, the engines had little difficulty in attaining a speed of 100 m.p.h., and *Drysllwyn Castle* succeeded in cutting the journey time to 93½ minutes as compared with the 105 minutes allowed. No extra fare is charged.

I consider that the public would prefer a generally high level of speed and punctuality throughout the system to a few trains running at 100 m.p.h. and over. It seems that the British Transport Commission has such a thing in mind. Take for example the counties of Lincoln, Norfolk and Suffolk. In these, the B.T.C. operates hundreds of diesel trains daily, trains which are fast, clean and punctual. Other parts of the country enjoy similar standards of travel and it is not exaggerating to say that we shall ultimately have the best railway system in the world. But we shall have to wait a little longer, and it is as well to remember that the French began to recondition their railways about 10 years before us.

F.G. Cockman
Bedford

21 OCTOBER 1959

SIR – I have been travelling over 30,000 miles each year by British Railways and on the Continent as far as Southern Spain, Southern Italy, Budapest and North Germany. Mr L.B. Nulty need have no fear that the soup will be spilled on either the Mistral or the Sud Express. The higher fares of special Continental expresses seem to be paid willingly, for the trains are always well filled.

Mr F.G. Cockman is too enthusiastic. In all my travels I have never yet timed 100 m.p.h., and only very few times just over 90 m.p.h. Speed and comfort by rail are both possible. In time we shall achieve both in Britain; at present the Continent is ahead.

G.R. Calvert
Oxhey, Herts

SIR – The *Brighton Belle* runs for passengers, not for prestige.

M. Macleod Carey
Hassocks, Sussex

DUE PRAISE

SIR – When travelling I am impressed by the great improvement in the catering services provided by British Railways, both on the trains and at stations, and feel that the public could help still further improve these services by passing on a word of encouragement whenever the circumstances called for it.

I mention this because of the gratitude with which words

of commendation from me have been received by catering staff whenever I have given them.

I think we are all too ready to rush into print with our complaints and not nearly so eager to pass on the much worthwhile compliments.

C.G. Gardiner
Ashtead, Surrey

6 FEBRUARY 1960
AN ENGINE-DRIVER'S SKILL

SIR — In these days when it is fashionable to grumble at British Railways, I would like to compliment them.

The *Aberdonian* on the night of Feb. 1 suffered a mishap to its engine. What might have been a nasty derailment became, owing to the skill of the driver, nothing but an annoying mechanical breakdown.

British Railways stopped the train at York, gave us a free breakfast, and also arranged to send off free telegrams for passengers. Also, they were prepared to transfer anyone who wished to a 'day' train.

Private enterprise could not have done more. It is a grave reflection that the driver of that train is paid about the same as a typist. I do not like that and hope it will be put right when the inquiry reports.

Viscount Stonehaven
London, SW7

23 JULY 1960
EATING ON THE TRAIN

SIR – In his article, 'Oh Dear, When Will British Railways Learn About Food?' Mr Egon Ronay is blaming the wrong people. Refreshment rooms and restaurant cars are the responsibility of the British Transport Hotels and Catering Services, over which British Railways have no control.

The article does raise the question as to whether it might not be better for the control of train meals to be in the hands of the railway operators. At least the complaints would be made to the right people.

There seems to be a good case for handing over operation of refreshment rooms to one of the many successful catering firms, or perhaps small private firms in each locality. We might then get genuine Banbury cakes at Banbury, Cornish pasties in Cornwall and real Yorkshire pudding when travelling up north.

Another possibility is for the refreshment rooms to be in the hands of corporation catering departments like that at Birmingham. Civic pride would then demand that each town would provide the best food for the hungry worker.

Whatever changes may take place in the course of time, let us always remember to place the blame where it really belongs. British Railways have troubles enough of their own.

R.J. Harbach
Press Officer, Midland Area, Railway Development Assn.
Solihull, Warwickshire

SIR – Having read Mr Egon Ronay's article on British Railways catering, may I say that food and service on the

British Railways diners are a little bit maligned? The food and service in the buffet cars, however, I find deplorable.

Why is catering on the B.R. steamers so excellent? I returned from a delightful cruise on the *Duke of Lancaster* which really was a luxury liner in miniature, and I looked in at the buffet car of the Ocean Express on my return journey from Southampton — it was truly disgusting.

(Mrs) M.F. Seidler
Ham Common, Surrey

SIR — Miss Beryl Hartland says: 'My thanks to French Railways for their car-sleeper express.' I doubt if Miss Hartland would have been quite so enthusiastic about French Railways, or Mr Egon Ronay so scathing about British Railways catering, if either of them had travelled on the Lyons–Boulogne car-sleeper express as I did last year and dined on the train.

It is a pity that Mr Ronay in particular did not have the opportunity of sampling the grey and soggy rice pilaff 'dusted' with liver from an unidentifiable animal, and the hard and greasy potatoes that were among the items on a menu costing more than twice as much as the price then charged for a four-course dinner on British Railways. It was, incidentally, almost midnight before all the harassed passengers had dined.

Perhaps French Railways advised Miss Hartland 'to dine in town before the train left at 8.30 p.m.', and took care that she did not travel in the same coach as I did, with its unflushable, evil-smelling lavatory!

D.S.W. Browne
Reigate, Surrey

25 JULY 1960

SIR — At the risk of flogging a dying horse, who incidentally refuses to budge, I hasten to endorse Mr Egon Ronay's illuminating article by my own experiences, which are almost identical.

They include the awful boat train meal (mine cost 15s) against which I warned my disbelieving and later rueful American friends; the revolting packed meals, so far the only alternatives to a 12s dinner that isn't worth the money (if it were, I would gladly pay it), and the indescribable refreshment rooms — Snow Hill, Birmingham, is a pretty example.

On the other hand, Paddington Station restaurant is excellent; so is the coffee served in containers on the platforms; so why isn't it drinkable in the dining cars? Is it used for the new diesel engines?

There are three solutions, besides Mr Ronay's one of emulating the airlines:

1 — To complain and complain, which few English people are willing to do.

2 — To order cold meat and salad, followed by cheese and biscuits and more salad — they can't cook that.

3 — To take one's own sandwiches.

Personally, I advocate all three.

Vivian Ellis
London, W8

26 JULY 1960

SIR – Let us be fair to British Railways. Mr Egon Ronay is, I feel, not.

As one who travels extensively all over the European railway network, I find that the present standard of British Railways catering service and 'new-look' buffets is not only admirable, but compares very favourably with Continental practice.

Incidentally, there is no trans-Europe express that goes from Ostend to Milan. The only T.E.E. train out of Ostend is the 'Safir', which goes to Frankfurt.

Merlin Minshall
President, Gastronomic Travellers Club
London, SW3

29 JULY 1960

SIR – Mr Vivian Ellis's statement that 'few English are willing to complain' is certainly not exaggerated.

I recently ordered, while travelling on British Railways, a toasted teacake. I was served from a pile on a tray with an utterly revolting specimen, dry and nearly cold.

I asked at once for a fresh one, immediately being eyed with distaste, almost enmity, by the entire company, who cast baleful glances in my direction as I awaited (for some considerable time) my delicious, freshly toasted 'new issue', dripping with butter.

Nell Cardew Mumford
London, N21

SIR – I can add a word to your correspondents' comments on railway catering. The coffee on the Ramsgate–Cannon Street business trains tastes of nothing but whatever sugar one puts in it and, faintly, cocoa.

D.R. Broome
Swalecliffe, Kent

30 JULY 1960

SIR – Whatever the relative standards of French and English restaurant car services, I do not think anyone can deny that the English railway station refreshment room has much to learn from its French counterpart.

'In France they order these things better' – and how much better! Until the day comes when a provincial railway station buffet can be recommended as one of the best eating places in the district, and even caters for wedding receptions – as happens in France – I think the British public are entirely right to complain of the appalling service they get, whoever is responsible for the catering.

We drink watery tea in cardboard cups and eat soggy rolls with a scrap of tasteless tinned ham in surroundings of squalor and disorder which languid West Indian attendants in dirty white coats are completely ineffectual to deal with.

Why should we put up with it any longer?

(Mrs) Maisie Pye-Smith
Corfe Castle, Dorset

7 JANUARY 1961
DIESEL'S DISGRACE

SIR – On Jan. 1 I started a journey to Paddington on a diesel-powered express from Penzance. Only a short while ago this train was powered by a steam engine of the Castle class to Plymouth, and by a King class from Plymouth to London. It was known as the *Cornish Riviera Express*.

It still bears the name, but it became evident before Plymouth that we were not quite maintaining the performance.

After Plymouth the burden proved too much for the diesel. It broke down near Westbury, and the task of hauling 14 full coaches to Paddington fell to a Castle-class engine.

The guard walked through the carriages saying we would be at least an hour late: the diesel had stranded the famous express for three-quarters of an hour. But a measure of atonement was offered by a noble performance of our new engine, and the train was only 40 minutes late.

Steam engines always did the journey so graciously. Surely a little coal could be spared so that the fame of this crack express could live on?

C.H. Salt
London, W12

25 JUNE 1961 (*Sunday Telegraph*)
HOW TO RUN A RAILWAY

SIR – If the railways need revenue, why not try collecting all the fares? I am assured by responsible railwaymen that dodgery by the public accounts for large sums, and that most of the dodges are known to the staff, but the organisation and manpower to stop them all are not there.

One travelling ticket collector told me that a day's work could bring in £20 to £30 in 'excess' fares — mostly from second-class passengers travelling first. What about those that get away?

T.R. Ford
London, SW19

5 SEPTEMBER 1961
DR BEECHING AND ROAD-RAIL PROBLEM

SIR — The choice of Dr Beeching will prove to be one of the major errors of policy committed by this Government. It transpires that his one preoccupation is to put the railways on a 'sound financial basis' — an impeccable phrase among business circles, but an irrelevant cliché to economists.

Dr Beeching is apparently oblivious to the real problem facing the nation: the choice between public and private transport, in particular the choice between the railways and private motoring.

The costs to the nation of the latter luxury far exceed anything the motorists, as a group, have to pay, even if we neglect many of the unsavoury consequences of the spread of motorised traffic. In effect, then, private motoring is receiving a vast subsidy at the expense of the nation.

To restore the balance our railways, like the French, should be heavily State-subsidised (or private motoring taxed to the extent necessary to cover the cost it incurs).

Thus Dr Beeching's 'ruthlessness' in attempting to cover costs — his raising of fares and closing down of 'unprofitable' branch lines — is completely mis-directed. It reduces the use made of public transport and adds further to the existing road congestion at a time when exactly the opposite policy is called for.

The nation's transport system is a major economic problem, and the Government has the obligation to seek advice from those economists in whose domain such a problem falls. Alas, one is left with the impression that the Government is trying to skirt this problem and to appease its conscience by paying a fancy salary to an administrator obviously bereft of any economic sophistication.

A salary of £24,000 a year may guarantee administrative ruthlessness, but it won't elicit a policy for the nation.

E.J. Mishan
London School of Economics

14 SEPTEMBER 1961
TRANSPORT OF FREIGHT MUST COME FIRST

SIR — Basic definitions at the London School of Economics must have changed since my day.

It is true, as Dr E.J. Mishan says, that the nation gives a vast subsidy to private motorists, but is that a reason for insisting that British Railways should give a vast subsidy to private com - muters? Pleasure, convenience, prestige and independence are far greater factors than economics in the increase of private motoring.

It is just not true that the crux of the transport problem lies in 'the choice between the railways and private motoring'. The crux of the problem lies in the movement of freight, not the carriage of passengers.

In the Nationalisation Act Parliament insisted that the railways should pay their way, taking one year with another. No one yet knows which part of the service is or can be viable, and which cannot. Dr Beeching is making it his first major job to find out.

When he does, he should publish his findings. If the Government then declares that some uneconomic services are socially necessary, the case for a straight subsidy to such services will be unanswerable.

But a blanket subsidy which might be used to cloak, and perhaps foster, inefficiency would be indefensible.

If the railways are to perform their essential function of transporting that proportion of the nation's freight which they are best fitted to carry, we must know which jobs they do best, and for that we must have the policy of commercial efficiency for which Dr Beeching is apparently striving.

A first-class railway system which can attract traffic is a national necessity, and when it is achieved we shall have the finest antidote to road congestion.

Lord Stonham
Chairman, Road and Rail Assn.
London, W1

From Brig. T.I. Lloyd

SIR – On transport matters Dr E.J. Mishan would have the Government consult the economists within whose domain the problems fall. The 1932 Government did better than that. It commissioned the four principal railway barons of the time (Walker, Stamp, Wedgwood and Milne) and four comparable road transport men, under the chairmanship of Sir Arthur (now Lord) Salter, to establish what would be fair play between rail and road.

Surely that problem was within the domain of these eight men? They decided that equity would be achieved when the revenue from motor taxation equalled the expenditure on road construction and maintenance.

Nowadays main taxation yields very much more than that, and in addition British Railways receive a subsidy of more than £2m. a week, but still Dr Mishan asserts that the railways are unfairly treated. He should first explain where the Salter Conference went wrong. How interesting it would be to observe him teaching those four railway men their business, even in retrospect.

T.I. Lloyd
Guildford, Surrey

17 SEPTEMBER 1961 (ST)

SIR – According to a paper read by Mr H.F. Brown at the end of last year, modernisation in the United States has proved a failure. Why is it supposed that we in this country can do better?

A great deal is expected of the Deltics and small wonder as they cost about five times as much as an ex-L.M.S. Duchess 4-6-2, the nearest approach to a Deltic in the matter of power, and its life is half as long.

B.R.'s record is not encouraging. King's Cross to Leeds in three hours is not particularly outstanding as the L.N.E.R. with its now despised Gresley Pacifics was covering the 185¾ miles in pre-war days in 162 minutes.

The diesel may yet prove to be little more than a terrifyingly expensive experiment. The Giesl Oblong Ejector invented by an Austrian engineer may vindicate the steam locomotive as being a more economic machine than the complicated and costly diesel.

N. Paddison
Neath, S. Wales

British Transport Commission comments: No one knows what a Duchess 4-6-2 would cost today. Deltics will go much faster with improved track conditions, and give many more hours' continuous service than any steam engine.

24 SEPTEMBER 1961 (ST)

A WORD FOR STEAM

SIR – British Railways' comment last week that diesels will go faster than steam engines and work for much longer continuous periods leaves me unconvinced.

There is no difference in the practical running speeds of steam, diesel and electric traction of equivalent power, though acceleration is better with the latter. In big countries triple-manned steam locomotives work trains for fifty or more hours continuously.

The choice between steam, electric and diesel traction is no longer a technical but an economic problem, which varies with conditions not only on different railways, but on the same railway. It is the relative costs of fuel, service, maintenance, depreciation and overheads per horse-power produced that is the deciding factor.

Those countries which produce cheap coal, like China and India, continue to build steam locomotives for general use, and confine other modes of traction to prescribed spheres because they find it pays them to do so.

D.S. Kent
London, SW1

1 OCTOBER 1961 (ST)

SIR – Although the steam locomotive may be capable of further technical improvement, the decision to abandon it is surely correct. The high price and scarcity of good quality coal, the public desire for cleaner travel, and the scarcity of labour for dirty and arduous work all point to it. The superior acceleration and climbing power of diesel and electric locomotives enable faster and more reliable schedules to be run.

Of the two, electric locos are undoubtedly superior in speed, tractive power, reliability and operating costs. But electrification involves very heavy capital expenditure on the line, particularly in built-up areas where bridges and tunnels must be altered to provide room for overhead wiring.

The B.R. modernisation scheme envisaged electrifying commuter services and the two most intensively used main lines, the West Coast route from Euston to the North, and the East Coast route from King's Cross. Dieselisation here was an interim measure and the locos will eventually be transferred to other lines, where electrification is not justified.

The costly American experience with main-line diesels and the French success with electrification show this was a correct decision.

Unfortunately, the Minister of Transport, Mr Marples, seems to think otherwise. The West Coast scheme was almost abandoned by the Government earlier this year and the East Coast scheme will probably now never be started. Modernisation generally is being slowed down with serious consequences for both the B.R. and for their manufacturers.

Fundamentally, of course, this reflects Mr Marples's own well-known antipathy to railways, and his faith in road transport. I believe this is a shortsighted policy which can only hamper the economy, clutter up the roads with even more lorries and prevent the railways ever serving the nation adequately.

Before he does any more harm Mr Marples should have a look at the remarkable achievement of the modernised French State Railways and the vital part they play in the booming French economy.

D. Alexander
Swindon, Wiltshire

25 NOVEMBER 1961
BRANCH LINES

SIR — When British Railways decide to close a branch line which is no longer economic do they take into consideration the consequent loss of business on the main lines?

I haven't travelled by train for years because indirect routes with changes caused by a closed line make it so inconvenient.

R.I.G. Reeve
Alverstoke, Hants.

5 JANUARY 1962
CANNOT RAILWAYS PLAN FOR COLD SPELLS?

SIR — Is it really necessary that a small snowfall, by Continental and Canadian standards, and a moderate frost should completely disrupt British Railways?

The same thing happened in 1959, 1960 and 1961 and will almost certainly happen in 1963. Is it beyond the management of British Railways to have a 'cold weather plan' so that it is prepared for annual aberrations in the weather?

An express train on Jan. 1 from Basingstoke to London took 3¼ hours to do the journey, for which the normal time is 50 minutes. On the return journey, by the 5 o'clock train, the passengers crowded in to capacity and had to wait in the station for one hour because there was no engine.

No one told passengers this fact on the loud-hailer, nor was there any senior member of the staff available to say when an engine was likely to be available or when the train would start. The conditions of squash as more and more passengers clambered aboard became almost unbearable. The journey again took more than three hours.

This total lack of communication with the public could not have been the fault of the weather. Someone at Waterloo must have known exactly what the situation was.

What a pity it is that the public is so passive and complains so little. But until it does it seems hard to see what is going to change British Railways' attitude to being prepared for cold weather rather than every year being surprised by it, with chaotic results.

K.M. Egleston
Basingstoke, Hants.

SIR – The dislocation of the railways, due largely to the freezing up of points, shows how vulnerable is the system in this country to icy conditions.

In Canada railway points have for years been treated with a dry graphite film. This needs renewing much less frequently than the grease used in this country, thus considerably reducing labour costs and helping to keep the points operating in the extreme conditions of recent days.

Several years ago we developed a similar graphite lubricant at the request of British Railways. It has been extensively and successfully tested, but little progress has been made with its adoption as normal practice.

It seems a pity that an opportunity to save money and to keep the trains running should be lost because of the extreme conservatism of British Railways' engineers.

R.M. Shrimpton
Man. Dir., Graphite Products Ltd.
London, SW18

28 JANUARY 1962 (ST)
LITTER LOUTS

SIR – On my return to Britain last week after a long holiday abroad I was immediately struck by the nauseating filthiness of main-line stations and trains. And as the fault lies not with British Railways but with the travelling public, who will scatter abroad chocolate-wrappers, cigarette-ends, ash and boxes, I suggest that the remedy lies in forbidding smoking on all trains, and in not selling sweets in stations. This may be a drastic measure, but it would not be undeserved.

Sandra Hill
London, SW13

11 FEBRUARY 1962 (ST)

SIR – With reference to Ann Dally's article 'If your children MUST smoke . . .'

The situation was nicely summed up in a non-smoking compartment recently. A man smoking a pipe got in, puffing clouds of the filth over everybody. When it was pointed out to him where he was, he glared and growled: 'You miserable lot ought to have brought your tambourines with you.' A gentleman in the carriage retorted, 'If you can't be happy without a dummy in your mouth, you ought to have brought your rattle as well.'

(Mrs) N. Gray
Wembley

17 FEBRUARY 1962
CABINED & CONFINED

SIR – I draw attention to a new peril on the railways. On four occasions recently, when travelling between Waterloo and Barnes, I have been unable to open the door to get out.

The first time I was swept on willy-nilly to the next station, while pondering whether to pull the communication cord. There, luckily, the platform was on the other side where the door opened easily. On the second occasion I managed, with great struggle, to open the window and thus turn the outside handle.

On the other two occasions fellow passengers, musclemen of enormous strength, managed either to open the door or to get the window down for the outside attack. Can nothing be done on behalf of the rest of us, or are we to regard railway carriages as mobile coffins?

L. Marsland Gander
London, SW13

3 MARCH 1962

SIR – We are sorry to hear about Mr L. Marsland Gander's troubles with our train door locks but, in fact, it is the result of deliberate action on our part.

Three years ago a girl passenger fell to her death when a door flew open. This demonstrated tragically that the very high standards of security on Southern Region door locks were not high enough to meet extreme tests. All our locks were as a result modified and it was necessary, among other things, to increase the pull required to operate them.

Although girls who were asked to test out the modified locks at our railway works had no difficulty in manipulating them, the extra stiffness – as we now know – can be inconvenient under practical service conditions.

The very punishing demands made on door locks on Southern Region trains make it extremely difficult to design a completely reliable lock which will meet the present safety requirements. Nevertheless, we shall continue to study the problem.

F.D.Y. Faulkner
Public Relations Officer, Southern Region, British Railways
London, SE1

L. Marsland Gander writes: I suggest a little oil. I now use the bus.

19 MARCH 1962
DIESEL FUMES AT STATIONS

SIR – Now that diesel engines are able to belch their poisons in the confined areas of railway termini, to be breathed in by a captive public, it might prove interesting if the medical experts conducted a survey among main-line station employees and regular travellers.

In her letter of March 14 Miss Doris Leslie (Lady Fergusson Hannay) points out that her husband, a non-smoker, died of lung cancer apparently contracted from driving behind road vehicles fuming into the relatively open air.

Trapped by a roof and by high walls, these fumes appear more menacing, especially if emitted by railway diesels of 2,000 or more horse-power. One has only to talk to porters at King's Cross to gain some practical information on the effect of such fumes on clothing, while Mr John Betjeman has drawn my attention to the erosion of ironwork and overhead girders from diesel exhaust.

K. Westcott Jones
London, SE25

30 JULY 1962
LAW & THE PORTER

SIR – I cannot help feeling that if Rule 10 of the British Transport Commission's by-laws concerning railwaymen were enforced at Waterloo Station, there would hardly ever be a porter on duty.

They would be daily at the police court answering summonses. For I know too well that when the businessmen's trains arrive from the west and disgorge stockbrokers, company directors and other gentlemen from Bournemouth and stations in the New Forest there is a rush of porters not only (a) to collect luggage but (b) to collect newspapers.

It is not uncommon to see a porter with a dozen under his

arm and usually a pink one in the pile. Whether they want to see their stocks and shares, use the papers for fire-lighting or pass them on to fried-fish shops, I do not know, but this is what happens.

Personally, I and a few of my friends give ours to the locomotive driver, who is glad of a reading respite from the hazards of train driving.

J.F.A. Frost
Southampton, Hants.

3 AUGUST 1962

SIR – I used to travel on a business train to Waterloo. Each morning the train was met by a particular railwayman who went through the train collecting all newspapers left by passengers.

Inquiries revealed that he came over to Waterloo from London Bridge specially to collect the papers off this train.

This practice suggested that (a) passengers to London Bridge either did not read newspapers, or, if they did, they did not leave them in the trains, and (b) perhaps more important, this particular individual ought to have been more usefully employed.

I am told that one day the train crew beat him to it and tore every newspaper in half!

V. Badman
Woking, Surrey

1 AUGUST 1962
DISCARDED RAILWAY COLOURS

SIR – I observe that the coaches forming such trains on the Western Region as the 'Cornish Riviera' and 'Torbay' expresses are no longer painted in the chocolate and cream colours of the old G.W.R.

Is this because Dr Beeching cannot bear to be reminded of a railway which gained the respect, and even the affection, of its employees and passengers – and consistently made a profit?

The Bishop of Crediton
Exeter

30 MARCH 1963
BEECHING BRITAIN

SIR – British Railways in their present state are surely a microcosm of Great Britain herself. That is, the basic shape of deployment is mid-Victorian, although random alteration and modernisation has been going on for years. Equally, British menial attitudes are like those of the pre-Beeching railways – traditional, unquestioning, rather than radical and analytical.

Is it not therefore time – in fact already late by 50 years – for us to do a Beeching on Great Britain as a whole? Should we not coldly analyse every aspect of our national deployment and our national institutions, and then ruthlessly replan to fit our true needs and opportunities? Has anyone, for example, actually ever costed the Sterling Area? *Does* it make us a profit? Or is it a source of weakness?

Every one of our most unquestioned institutions and habits should be subjected to ruthless analysis of the Beeching kind.

Although we are 50 years late, it may still not be too late.

Correlli Barnett
East Carleton, Norfolk

SIR – Dr Beeching hopes to avoid the railways' deficit by closing branch lines. But he gives no estimate of the cost to the nation of extra wear and tear to roads, nor of increased travelling times. Delays could be reduced by integrating the timetables of buses and trains, and seeing that they share stations, but there has been no hint of that.

Without a similarly comprehensive report on road transport it is impossible to judge the true cost to the nation of Dr Beeching's plan. There is as yet no evidence that it represents a net saving to the national economy.

A. Sandison
Chairman, South Croydon Liberal Assn.
Croydon, Surrey

SIR – Dr Beeching appeared on television as a giant among pigmies. His directness and clear-sightedness was as light to darkness. The muddied thinking of London University dons and professional economists was exposed by such simple and gentle logic that they were made to appear as juveniles before a tolerant instructor.

Dr Beeching will almost certainly be obstructed by politicians and trade unionists and other sectional interests. *If* left alone he would surely succeed in his objective, to the lasting benefit of this country.

Peter Crichton
Naunton, Glos.

SIR – One of the stations listed for closure in Dr Beeching's plan for the railways is Finchley Road and Frognal. The redecoration of this station was completed about a week ago. Even the brickwork has been repointed.

Patrick J. Davidson
London, W3

1 APRIL 1963

SIR – How sorry one feels for Dr Beeching. Here is a man of undoubted abilities who has been given a job in which it would appear he is not allowed to exercise any imagination or constructive ability, but has been employed solely to produce a superb thesis on a second-hand dogma.

Looking back over many years the basic pattern of railway policy has been unchanging – as they lost money they closed lines and increased fares, which resulted in losing more money to induce them to close more lines and increase more rates to lose still more money.

To allow more and more existing assets to fall into disuse would not be tolerated by any sound business concern. Ideas would be encouraged to find a means of making 'profitable use of them'; possibly it would need revolutionary ideas, but a man of real vision and ability could surely find them.

It would be very interesting to learn whether Dr Beeching has any ideas of his own apart from the dictated policy he has so ably expounded, and whether anyone else connected with the compilation of the report has proposed anything constructive in a minority report.

W. de L. Marshall
Eccleshall, Staffs.

SIR – One thing Dr Beeching's excellent report has exposed – the railways are not to be run for the benefit of the public, but to provide jobs for members of various trade unions. There is to be no redundancy, however inefficient they are. If Dr Beeching's exposition of the situation is adopted, the unions are threatening to take strike action. Was there ever a more blatant example of a minority holding a majority to ransom?

In spite of our so-called advance in education, we haven't progressed much since the mob wrecked Ackroyd's (sic.) 'Spinning Jenny'.

J. Alan Goddard
London, WC2

SIR – You report that Mr Macmillan is to lose his home station, Horsted Keynes. As senior porter at this station for some years I should like to say that I have never yet seen the Rt. Hon. Gentleman at our station, so I fail to see that its closure, regretted as at is, will make the slightest difference to him.

Frederick Miles
Birchgrove, Sussex

3 APRIL 1963

BRANCHES THAT FEED THE MAIN LINES

SIR – Dr Beeching's plan has apparently been drawn up with the sole object of reducing expenditure on the railways without considering its effect on other means of transport and the country as a whole. No doubt he has masses of figures to support his plan, but I have travelled some 360,000 miles by rail all over Great Britain from Penzance to the Highlands, so am not altogether unacquainted with the problems involved.

The pruning of lengthy branch lines serving mainly rural areas and the closing of small stations on main lines are undoubtedly economically desirable, but surely it is wrong to cut off so many holiday resorts from any communication except by roads already greatly overcrowded in the summer months.

It is proposed to spend millions of pounds on modernising the main lines, but, bereft of the branch lines which feed them, some of the main lines would soon cease to pay their way. An outstanding example is the present main line from Waterloo to Exeter and Plymouth. This passes through few large centres of population, but by means of its branch lines serves many popular seaside resorts in Devon and Cornwall. Under Dr Beeching's proposals the main line apparently stops short at Okehampton and loses all its branch lines. In those conditions it is difficult to see how it could possibly pay its way.

It is probable that much of the traffic from Waterloo to Devon and Cornwall would be lost to British Railways permanently. Rather than take a train to the nearest station to their destination and then change to a bus for a further journey of anything up to 30 miles (in the case of Bude, for instance), many holiday-makers may prefer to do the whole journey by road. Much additional road transport for both passengers and goods will be required, and the effect on the road traffic in Devon and Cornwall during the summer is likely to be chaotic.

Many other areas have similar problems. One wonders, for instance, what will happen to the port of Stranraer if it finds itself 51 miles from its nearest railway station at Ayr. Minehead, Buxton, Whitby and Skegness are other resorts which will be far from a railway, and the economic effect on them could be disastrous.

R. Excell
Bromley, Kent

SIR – In 1961 42 people (passengers, railwaymen and others) were killed in train accidents, and III were seriously injured, while on the roads in the same year 6,908 people were killed and 84,936 seriously injured. These figures are taken from *Whitaker's Almanack* for 1963.

If Dr Beeching's plan is carried out, and large numbers of passengers are diverted from the railways to the roads, it seems certain that each year many of them will be killed or seriously injured who would otherwise have travelled safely on the railways. Did Mr Marples consider this aspect of the plan before deciding to back it whole-heartedly?

C.J. Ware
Beckenham, Kent

SIR – It has been suggested that many of the rail routes to be abandoned may be made into roads, but this may not be practicable with some of the smaller (and often more picturesque) stretches, for instance, in Devon or Cornwall.

Could not a few of these be maintained as foot or bridlepaths by joint action on the part of the many organisations devoted to rambling, pony-trekking, the preservation of wildlife, and so on? They are not likely to be commandeered for missile ranges!

F.H.W. Hawes
Dagenham, Essex

4 APRIL 1963

WHY NOT THE RAIL BUS?

SIR – When Parliament is digesting the Beeching report, and local authorities and private citizens are looking for alternatives to railway coaches, they should not overlook the rail bus.

I remember hiring a rail bus from the Stationmaster of Amman in 1956 and driving to Maan when the desert was impassable to motor traffic. With a driver and mechanic-guard the return journey over 260 miles of railway track, with overnight halt, cost £16. The bus, diesel-driven, was of North British construction.

I recollect that by accepting several Bedouin travellers on the return journey we defrayed the cost of the venture.

Rail buses could serve loop lines and spurs cleared of heavier traffic by the Beeching retrenchment. They could stop at halts where no railway staff was maintained. Ours was versatile enough to avoid stray camels and goats. It could be the answer for branch-line commuters.

Ian Colvin
London, SW1

SIR – Does anyone in his right senses imagine that people travel into London by public transport (or by car for that matter) during the rush hour because they like it? Yet we hear it said that the increase in fares has brought no appreciable reduction in the number of people travelling.

It is like hitting a prisoner chained hand and foot and then saying he doesn't mind it because he doesn't hit back. All most people can do is to give up their job!

J.S. Watson
Bushey Heath, Herts.

10 APRIL 1963
IRRESPONSIBLE RAIL STRIKE BEFORE DECISION

SIR – The threat by the executive of the National Union of Railwaymen to strike on account of Dr Beeching's plan is a further demonstration of their utter irresponsibility.

It is difficult to see what they are striking about. Dr Beeching has produced a very brilliant report, giving his ideas of what is required over a period of time to provide an efficient and paying service. I do not suppose for one moment that Dr Beeching expects his report to be put into operation in its entirety, and in any event it is up to the Government of the day to decide to what extent and over what period of time the report will be implemented.

When such a decision is reached is surely the time to protest, but certainly not now, when nothing has happened except for one man to give his opinion as to what is the best course for the future.

I would have thought other unions might have learnt a lesson from those associated with the shipyards, whose actions over the past 10 years have been responsible for such delays in delivery and increases in price that ship owners now go elsewhere for repairs and construction.

As a result the shipyards are short of work, for which the unions are largely to blame.

J.G. Rutter
London, W1

SIR – Having read your leader 'Railway Union Threats', I feel that criticism must also be laid against Dr Beeching.

Mr Sidney Greene advises us that neither he nor other union leaders were consulted or advised about the recent Beeching plans prior to their being made public. Surely, with such drastic action as he intends taking, Dr Beeching should have consulted with the union leaders, advising them of his proposals, and explained to them his reasons for such closures and redundancies.

Mr Greene and his colleagues are intelligent people and realise that the railways are in need of modernising. It is also still fresh in their minds that on the last occasion when redundancies were announced they were not consulted; this led to strike action.

It would be a good thing if Dr Beeching realised that the unions are a powerful body, and all they have asked is to be consulted before such decisions are made public.

Jeffrey Fox
Edgware, Middlesex

29 JUNE 1963
HOLIDAY HOMES

SIR – If the coaches that the British Railways Board is proposing to burn to dispose of its surplus rolling stock were to be placed on disaffected railway lines in the vicinity of abandoned railway stations (*i.e.*, with villages, shops, etc. not far away) could they not be profitably adapted as dwellings?

If the sites were well chosen, I feel that enterprising builders could do much to make such communities attractive, and inexpensive, either as holiday accommodation or as more permanent homes for the retired.

In the case of a location close to the sea, for example, I should certainly be prepared to have my name added to the list of those interested in such a scheme. Many others of your readers may well feel the same way.

Mary Williamson
Paris

2 SEPTEMBER 1963
RAIL CLOSURES COST

SIR – Thank you for your lively but balanced editorial of Aug. 19 headed provocatively 'Stonham v Beeching'.

You rightly insist that judgement must be based on facts and figures. My Council's view, confirmed by the facts that are available, is that the published figures are either false or misleading. For example, on page 16 of his report Dr Beeching puts revenue at 2d per mile, but on pages 97–99 he gives the figure of earnings and passenger miles on three branch lines, and on his own figures the passenger-mile earnings work out at from 1.1d to 1.3d per mile. Obviously therefore his total earnings figures are in one case only just over half, and the other cases two-thirds, of what they really are. Such enormous errors make us extremely uneasy because they could make all the difference between closing a line and keeping it running.

Dr Beeching declares that branch-line closures will save at least £30m. This works out an average of £13,000 a year for every station he proposes to close. This is a vastly higher figure than the prospective saving on any line (dividing the line saving by the number of stations) for which British Railways have published figures. And that is assuming that we accept their figures at face value.

This obviously we cannot do, because the figures now

being sent to Transport Users' Consultative Committees are not figures of branch-line takings or earnings, but of 'revenue attributable to the line'.

This is an artificial figure arrived at by a secret formula. It is composed of only that part of a line's takings which are attributable to journeys over the branch plus a similar branch allow - ance for tickets purchased outside for destinations to the line.

In the cases which we have been able to investigate (with great difficulty) the branch takings alone exceed British Railways' artificial 'revenue attributable' figure, and of course there must be added the value of tickets purchased outside. Almost all these earnings, not just a proportion of them, would be lost to the railways if the line closes.

Dr Beeching says that the Board makes an honest assessment of the loss of income to main lines arising from a branch-line closure, but why does he not include this in the figures to the T.U.C.C.? Better still, why not show all the income to which a branch line gives rise so that everyone can see how it compares with the costs?

Above all why not, in addition to giving the *present* movement and terminal costs of a line (which are still mostly on a scale appropriate to heavy traffic), tell the T.U.C.C. and the public what the costs would be if the tracks, stations (or halts), signals, sidings, locomotives, coaches and staff were streamlined to the level required for a lightly used line?

With this information it would be possible to see that justice was being done. Without it we shall continue to believe that we are being asked to accept something which is not in the interests of the nation or the travelling public.

Lord Stonham
Chairman, National Council on Inland Transport
London, EC4

17 SEPTEMBER 1963

'INDOMITABLE REFUSAL' TO TRAVEL BY TRAIN

SIR – During a railway career of almost 40 years I have served as a relief station-master on 21 separate branch lines and until quite recently as a resident station-master on a line now under imminent threat of closure. I have therefore followed Lord Stonham's anti-closure campaign with unfailing interest, if not always with a like degree of comprehension.

Bluntly, to the experienced observer his knowledge of these matters seems to be in inverse ratio to his readiness to debate them. His repeated allegations that the railways support their closure proposals with incorrect and deliberately misleading statistics only serve to confirm this assessment of his qualifications to comment, as he does with such uninhibited freedom, on this aspect of railway policy.

My experience of branch-line traffic surveys has been two-sided. Occasionally I assisted in the survey as an investigator: more often the boot was on the other foot, and I was in charge of the station being put under the microscope.

This I can say without fear of contradiction: every investigation was thorough, impartial and aimed only at providing a true picture of the current traffic position. There was no angling, no fiddling and no figure juggling. The facts, extracted from the station records, were left to speak for themselves. That these facts frequently told a sonorously doleful tale of falling revenues and diminishing traffic levels was no fault of the investigators, and no doubt was outside the immediate scope of their briefing.

Incidentally – and this must be emphasised – these traffic inquiries were, and still are, an essential part of any closure sequence. They are repeated, not once but many times before an eventual decision is made, and it is only when the position is obviously irretrievable that the axe is applied.

The withdrawal of non-paying passenger services and the closing of redundant stations is by no means a feature peculiar to the Beeching era. The process began many years ago: tentatively perhaps, and at the outset most certainly timidly. In accelerating matters the 'Dreadful Doctor' is merely substituting common sense for timidity by putting into action theories and convictions long held by many railwaymen.

It behoves everyone to preserve a sense of proportion on this closure question. It is not Dr Beeching who is closing the branch lines and stations. It is the massive, cheerful and indomitable refusal of the public to use them which is doing that. He is merely taking a hint which for the past 10 years at least has been broad enough for any reasonable person to accept.

I have considerable, and recent, experience of working on a 'threatened' rural line.

No sooner is it known that closure is contemplated than a trickle of letters, most enclosing a postal order for 1s or 2s, begins to arrive from railway enthusiasts in far distant parts, each asking for information, comments, specimen tickets, mementoes, photographs and what-have-you. One replies non-committally – as the letters range from the reasonably level-headed to the wildly zany – and in the matter of relics, keepsakes and near-free samples of the ticket stock, sometimes at some small pecuniary disadvantage.

But apart from the automatic objection from the local authorities, other reaction in the affected area is nil – or at most it is confined to a little gentle leg-pulling of the 'they've-tumbled-to-you-at-last' variety.

The simple truth is that the locals, and this goes for 99.9 per cent of them, could not care less whether their line lives or dies. Despite what Lord Stonham may say, they have moved gaily and whole-heartedly into the exhilarating age of the motor-car — and that is where they are firmly resolved to stay. Many are car owners, or if they are not then the 'spare-seat' freemasonry common to all rural districts is sufficient to meet their transport needs.

S. Scott
Whitley Bay, Northumberland

27 November 1963
TRAVEL LAWS

SIR — I read in your issue of Nov. 20 of the young man fined for travelling in a Ladies Only compartment on a train although the lady occupant invited him to use it.

I wish British Railways would be as zealous in prosecuting those selfish nuisances who persist in smoking in non-smoking compartments irrespective of the wishes of other travellers.

Incidentally, why not Men Only compartments where men can retreat from the huge bags, umbrellas and empty chatter of female travellers?

W.B. Smith
London, N10

22 JANUARY 1964
BRITISH STATIONS

SIR — I have just returned to London after visiting Southern France and Italy, and I took a special interest in their lovely stations.

Visiting Genoa, Florence and Rome, I went into their refreshment rooms and bars in the evening where all was clean and tidy, while even the steps approaching the stations were swept at 8.15 in the evening. I visited Nice and also two Paris stations, and found them just as clean as the Italian ones.

Imagine my disgust when I arrived back in London and had to walk through Waterloo. The station was just one mass of litter, old food and rubbish strewn everywhere – and no sign that anyone had made the slightest effort to sweep it up. I must say that as an Englishwoman I was deeply ashamed of what I saw.

Nora E. Lassen
Sunningdale, Berks.

21 JUNE 1964 (ST)
TO A STANDSTILL?

SIR – Dr Beeching has reduced the railways' annual deficit by £22 million. But he has achieved this only by carrying his policy of closing down railway services to a ridiculous extreme. At a time when Mr Marples is studying ways of alleviating traffic congestion Dr Beeching is threatening such busy suburban services as Liverpool to Southport, Manchester to Buxton and London (Broad Street) to Richmond.

It has been said locally that if the Liverpool–Southport line closes the only way into the centre of Liverpool will be over the tops of the cars on the road.

Peter Blackburn
Crosland Moor, Yorks.

28 JUNE 1964 (ST)
BEECHING'S FAILURES

SIR – Does Ian Waller really feel it a 'dramatic speed-up' when ten minutes is cut off the pre-war schedule of a 225-mile run? ('Mixed Bag for Beeching', June 21).

Can it be other than pathetic when a 100 m.p.h. sign is erected along a line where only a handful of locomotives can reach this speed? And does not 500 or 5,000 runs at a bit over 60 m.p.h. have to be seen not only against the promise of the modernisation scheme, but also in relation to the astronomical sums spent to get this result?

That promise was for freight speeds of 50–55 m.p.h. average – no more than a dream these days – while passenger trains were to cover main runs at 70–75 m.p.h., a figure which at least one General Manager would reckon too low to be competitive?

Where are they? We'll see something of the kind when the West Coast electrification is completed. Then results should be not far below the French but with lighter trains. On the other lines the sheer inadequacy of locomotive power will prevent anything like it.

Against 3,680 h.p. of the electrics the best the diesels can show is about a thousand less for the few 'Deltics' and some 1,400 h.p. less for the Class 4 now being ordered in large numbers. This ordering a boy to do a man's job seems to me one of the biggest of the Beeching failures.

L. Irvine-Brown
Malpas, Cheshire

SIR – Now that British Railways have turned the corner would it be too much to ask Dr Beeching for a wash-basin in the

'Ladies' at Holyhead terminal station? We don't ask for hot water; cold would be better than the present condition of no water at all – except in the 'pull and let go'.

C.E. Holmes
Newcastle upon Tyne

25 SEPTEMBER 1964
BRITISH RAIL

SIR – Residents in this part of Dorset will appreciate British Railway's desire to change the name to 'British Rail', as we have now only one railway serving this area instead of three, and that line is now nine miles away at Bournemouth.

A.E. Green
West Moors, Dorset

28 APRIL 1965
HOOLIGANS ON THE RAILWAY

SIR – After the Great Train Robbery heavy prison sentences were imposed on the culprits in order, so we are told, to deter others.

Are we to wait until a major train disaster actually *occurs* before we take effective action about the current vandalism on the railways? Now, surely, is the time (and not after the event) to announce to all who may be contemplating these acts of violence just what they may expect.

The admonitions of magistrates, short prison sentences and minor fines are no way to curb the wave of brutality which is sweeping through our society to-day. Such things only cause the thugs and hooligans, the undisciplined children and their irresponsible parents to thumb their noses at so-called authority and to make the perpetrators appear as heroes in the eyes of their associates.

It is high time we took the word 'punishment' from the back of the cupboard, where it has been for so long, and brought it back into every-day usage. It is a fundamental mistake to give the type of person who goes in for this sort of activity the impression that authority has 'gone soft'.

If train robbers are given 30 years, I see no reason why potential mass-murderers (for that is what they are), or those responsible for them, should get away with the puny sentences which they may enjoy to-day.

Barbara Peake
London, SE5

17 JUNE 1965
BARON BRADSHAW

SIR — Dr Beeching's title surely should not be Baron Bradshaw, but Baron Lines.

(Mrs) M.H. Wooding
Ewell, Surrey

26 FEBRUARY 1966
UCKFIELD LINE

SIR — You report under the heading 'Farewell trip by steam train' (Feb. 2) that the Uckfield line is to be closed.

This is far from being the case: British Railways have made certain proposals to the Minister under the 1962 Transport Act. But with the growing use of this line by London commuters and others for local and cross-country travel from the Kent lines to the South coast it is surely inconceivable that any responsible Minister would allow these proposals to proceed on planning grounds.

Added to this there is the increasing road congestion, with neighbouring lines, as much as 12–14 miles distant, already past saturation point and the fact that the route serves as an alternative in emergency to the main London, Brighton, Newhaven and Eastbourne lines.

We may have said goodbye to steam, but the railway must surely continue to serve us, as it has done for more than 100 years, until the Minister can devise some better means of travel.

A.R. Mordaunt
Acting Sec., East Sussex Travellers Assn.,
Buxted, Sussex

2 MARCH 1966

SIR – Your correspondent who would keep the Uckfield line to avoid road congestion must be joking. Its level crossing at Uckfield closes the busy London–Eastbourne trunk road for about 15 minutes at a time, and I have known the resultant traffic jam build up to four miles long at holiday weekends.

One sits waiting for at least 10 minutes while the train appears to have died in the adjacent station. When eventually it does venture over the level crossing, it is most unusual for it to contain as many as five shadowy figures in its tattered coaches. One is left for several more minutes to wonder how many of these are passengers and how many are railway employees.

John E.H. Stretton
London, SW13

29 APRIL 1966
INJURY AND INSULT

SIR – The Bowling club in Dalry, Kirkcudbrightshire (of which I am a member) received from British Railways recently a brochure with a covering letter exhorting us to use British Rail when travelling to fulfil sports fixtures.

It would seem that the railway authorities are as yet unaware that the county of Kirkcudbright is entirely without railway facilities, thanks to Dr Beeching. The nearest passenger station to this village is Dumfries, a matter of 26 miles away.

Joseph Barber
Dalry, Kirkcudbrightshire

2 SEPTEMBER 1966
THE NEW LOGIC

SIR – On purchasing a cup of tea at King's Cross station recently I was charged 7d, an increase of 16.6 per cent on the previous price.

On complaining to the cashier I was floored by her reply. 'We have been forced to do this by the Government's prices and incomes freeze.'

R.W. King
Ewell, Surrey

10 SEPTEMBER 1966
RUNAWAY ENGINE

SIR – It is reported in your columns (Sept. 6) that a locomotive, by its own volition, ran away from Carnforth, and was not overtaken for nine miles.

I have it on record that in October, 1859, an almost exactly similar incident took place on the London, Brighton & South Coast Railway, when early one morning a locomotive (unattended) gently puffed its way out of the shed at Petworth, and was not arrested until a courageous railways servant swung himself on to the footplate and shut off the regulator.

Is it not time that British Railways learned the lesson?

A.C. Johnstone
Ruislip, Middlesex

15 SEPTEMBER 1966

SIR – Mr. A.C. Johnstone (Sept. 10) is quite correct, I believe, in his recollection of the unattended nomadic engine at Petworth in 1859. But he omitted to add that when it was recaptured some miles away near Pulborough the front buffers were found to be gaily festooned with four or five sets of level-crossing gates.

Hilary Cripps
Worthing, Sussex

21 SEPTEMBER 1966

SIR – Mr Hilary Cripps (Sept. 15) has rightly commented on my omission in relation to the adornment of the Petworth (1859) locomotive by crossing gates on the buffer beam. But, sir, I made a much more serious omission in failing to mention that she steamed for 17½ miles before being brought to a standstill.

A.C. Johnstone
Ruislip, Middlesex

24 SEPTEMBER 1966

SIR – Books on railway history disclose a more serious state of affairs than your correspondents suggest. There were at least five runaway engines between 1849 and 1936, and except for one fatality at Donnington in 1849 they make amusing reading. But the runaways must have seemed anything but funny to the railwaymen concerned and the engines were brought to a standstill by acts of great courage.

Having had our joke let's be fair. Five engines at large in 87 years – a wonderful record when you consider that there were 20,000 steam engines in service.

F.G. Cockman
Bedford

28 SEPTEMBER 1966

SIR – I found both Mr A.C. Johnstone's and Mr Hilary Cripps's letters very interesting. The engine running away to Horsham on that October day in 1859 may have caused embarrassment to the London, Brighton and South Coast Railway Company. The branch line had been open for just over a week!

The lines closed four months ago, but the incident of the runaway engine was the first of many funny incidents that occurred on the Midhurst line.

I am compiling the history of the Midhurst branch line, and if any of your readers have photographs or information of this historic railway I would be pleased to hear from them.

Andrew S. Benson
Taylor's Cottage, Chichester Road, Midhurst, Sussex

2 JANUARY 1967
FRANCE'S 'AERO TRAIN'

SIR — I was most interested to read your report that the French are developing an 'aero train' which runs on air cushions on an overhead track, and that a network of such trains linking the main cities of France is being planned. Only a few months ago British Railways, I understand, stated that they were not interested in air cushion trains because 'they had no future'.

And so, as with the VTOL (vertical take-off and landing) supersonic fighter and the swing-wing aeroplane, we are once more failing to exploit our inventions to the full, and just sitting back watching other countries develop our ideas. In due course no doubt, and at enormous expense, we will be forced to buy equipment from these foreign countries incorporating our ideas developed by them. Equipment which we could so easily have built ourselves with great saving in time and money.

A few years ago someone said that 'what this country lacks

is talent which recognises talent'. This becomes more apparent every day.

It will be recalled that before the war a well-known scientist did not see any use for radar, and even after the war another scientist, also in an influential position, was against this country building a supersonic aeroplane.

It is quite clear that we analyse our inventions incorrectly and those people who have to make decisions are being badly advised. Frequently we spend vast sums on projects which are subsequently cancelled.

A new organisation is required consisting of far-sighted and practical men who will thoroughly examine all inventions placed before them. Degrees of priority must be determined so that the necessary backing can be given to those showing great promise. The air cushion train must be placed high on the list – and quickly too.

Air Vice-Marshal V. S. Bowling
St Florence, Pembs.

8 MARCH 1968

WHERE ONE TRACK IS ENOUGH

SIR – You record (Feb. 24) that there is a proposal afoot to reduce at least one section of rail line, Wolverhampton to Chester, to single track. Does this mean that the influence of a practical railwayman at the top is already having its effect? It has long been absolutely preposterous that so much double track has been retained in areas where there has been no justification for the past 20 years; yet British Railways have been allowed to quote the costs of such excess trackage as a reason for closures.

The latest line is the Perth–Aberdeen line through the

Vale of Strathmore which could have been singled years ago and retained as an alternative in case of blockage of the coast route. Do Carlisle to Edinburgh, Newcastle to Edinburgh, or even Carlisle to Glasgow routes require two tracks when all local services have gone?

Or is it that the unreliability of modern motive power makes it difficult to achieve any sort of dependable service?

L. Irvine-Brown
Malpas, Cheshire

19 APRIL 1968

LEVEL CROSSING RISKS

SIR — Every time there is an accident on an unmanned level crossing there is a public outcry against these installations. However we should not finally admit that the Briton is incapable of dealing with a simple procedure which his Continental counterpart takes for granted.

The fundamental reason for these accidents is unfamiliarity on the part of British motorists with the procedure to be adopted when the signal starts to flash.

There would be far fewer incidents if the present flashing signals were normal traffic lights, with green, amber and red lamps, and a well-defined 'stop' line — and if the crossing of the red light were made an offence, as it is at any other cross-roads. Our drivers are used to stopping for this type of signal, and such a modification would overcome the fatal hesitation and uncertainty caused through unconditioned reflexes.

The simple answer is often the most effective one.

Robert Heard
Maidstone, Kent

SIR – Would not the use of burglar-alarm-type lights and receivers used diagonally across the tracks and connected to the railway signals warn engine drivers that 'Continental type' level crossings were obstructed?

H.W. Haskins
Tavistock, Devon

SIR – Considering the quite unbelievable lack of safeguards at 'Continental' type crossings compared with the safeguards built into the railway signalling system, it seems as if it doesn't matter what a train runs into as long as it isn't another train!

A.C. Phillips
Basingstoke, Hants.

SIR – Surely the danger at automatic level crossings would be greatly reduced were the barriers to be positioned further from the railway tracks, say 30 yards or more. This would enable any traffic caught inside the automatic barriers to stay in safety well away from the passing train.

W. Thomas-Ellam
Eastbourne, Sussex

SIR – Hixon and Easter entirely apart, may I suggest British Rail make an immediate order that every locomotive approach these level crossings only at a speed enabling it to stop before it if there is an obstruction.

I appreciate this would cause rail delay, but death must come first until British Rail make these crossings safe.

T.B. Flewitt
Nottingham

SIR — Your leader states that 24 seconds are allowed for motorists to go across an unmanned level crossing. In Scotland last year I towed a caravan across one of these Russian roulette crossings and I had only five seconds. The express was in sight when the barrier came down. The rear of the caravan was almost struck by the arm of the barrier.

D. Halliday
Leeds

24 APRIL 1968

SIR — So any action regarding Continental-type level crossings is to await the report of a public inquiry, which, with commendable urgency, will re-open on April 29! 'The inquiry . . . still has to hear considerable technical evidence . . . '

There are two items of evidence now available which render all others irrelevant as far as the continued use of these crossings in their present form is concerned.

The first is that the safety of rail traffic is no longer dependent upon trained and supervised rail staff but upon members of the whole general public, with its inevitable element of the illiterate, the careless, and those not in full possession of mental or physical faculties, either temporarily or congenitally. In no other case of public transport of large numbers is this so. It also depends upon the whims of the internal combustion engine.

Secondly. Whatever the statistical probability of these cros - sings becoming blocked that was assumed when their use was considered, there is now ample evidence that it was wrong.

Any concern other than a nationalised industry whose system or product caused 16 deaths in four months would be promptly, and rightly, closed down by the authorities.

These crossings must be manned, either permanently or until such time as they can be modified to give a degree of safe operation.

P.R. Hall
Brighton

7 MAY 1968

SIR – After the recent appalling accidents and the numerous reports of near misses Mr Henry Johnson, Chairman of the British Railways Board, will have difficulty in convincing the public that the new Continental-type level crossings are as safe as the old manned crossings.

He says soothingly that the degree of risk in the new crossings is 'acceptable'. Acceptable to whom, I pray? Only to Mr Johnson, I imagine.

M.C. Blakeman
London, SE20

29 SEPTEMBER 1968 (ST)
PLEASE DROP ME

SIR – As a student 18 years ago I was a temporary porter at Cannon Street station and it appears that conditions and attitudes have not changed. Immigrants have nothing to do with the problem for there were none then.

Our engagement as extra Christmas staff was quite unnec - essary since we, and all the 'regulars', spent most of the night shift in the rest room playing cards or frying sausages on the corner gas ring. When there was a train to off-load we soon learnt the vans to go for were those with boxes of flowers not the ones packed to their roofs with heavy luggage.

No one cared about anything, whether it was an expensive suitcase, a plant, or a carton of fruit. And as for consignments labelled 'Fragile', 'Glass' or 'This Way Up' these were read as 'Please Drop Me'.

Cannon Street is a commuter's station, so there were few tipping travellers. Waterloo, though, that was the place to be at Christmas time. It was there my night shift mates spent their day. All they needed was a cap.

J.G. Parkins
Kingston-upon-Thames

7 JUNE 1969
LINES WHICH DO NOT PAY

SIR – The reason given for closing branch railway lines is that they do not pay.

When they are closed, whole communities in the districts depending on them complain of being deprived of their services.

Instead of simply closing the line why do British Railways not try the alternative of charging higher rates on these lines for a trial period?

They might find rail users willing to pay more to retain what they consider an essential service.

P.F. Hesketh
Hale, Lancs.

16 AUGUST 1969
WHERE TROUSERS GO

SIR – I recently travelled to London from Perth, on the car/sleeper service. I have used this service on many occasions, and have always found the furnishings of the sleeper adequate. On this occasion, for the first time, I found that the non-removable coat-hangers attached to the walls had no built-in bars on which to hang my trousers, nor was there any other fitting for the purpose.

I inquired from the attendant who assured me that it was now the policy of British Rail to fit bars to coat-hangers only in first-class sleepers and not in second-class, or one-class as on the car/sleeper service.

Might one inquire from British Rail on what grounds they made the momentous decision that only first-class passengers should wear trousers?

Or is the omission of the trouser bars one of their major economies designed to reduce their annual deficit?

J.F. Todhunter (Lt.-Col.)
Bures St Mary, Suffolk

4 JANUARY 1971
RAIL FOOD THAT SHOULD BE DENATIONALISED

SIR – It is arguable whether it is the right time or desirable to auction the properties of the BBC. After all, the BBC was at its best under Lord Reith when it was a monopoly. Since then it has deteriorated and there is little to choose between it and its sordid commercial rival, whose advertising activities must be inflationary. The more widespread they become, the more anti-social will be the results. But there are not lacking other aspects of nationalised industry that could be hived off tomorrow morning with advantage to all.

High priority should be given to restaurant cars of British Rail. At a time when food is generally improving in Britain, the worst meals at the price, apart from breakfast, in the kingdom are available to those whose misfortune is to be in need of food while travelling by train. Meals of identically inferior quality, excluding pudding, can be obtained in the Pullman car from London to Liverpool for 29s, or in the ordinary restaurant car plus pudding for 19s 6d plus 2s for a cup of coffee. This is, of course, in addition to the supplementary charge for the Pullman.

A discriminating patron would return similar food at a similar price to the kitchen if he were a free agent in a commercial and static restaurant. Afternoon teas are no less expensive, bread and a scraping of butter being provided off salvers as if they were delicatessen. Chocolate biscuits when available are rationed. The choice of sandwiches and other offerings in the buffet car deteriorates steadily. On Sundays, passengers are expected to starve.

Surely it is time that the captive travelling public, instead of being exploited by the sadistic British Rail, was afforded the opportunity of increasing the profits of a private catering contractor, of whom there is no shortage, interested in expansion into a new and potentially profitable field. As a sop, the Railway Hotels might be thrown in the package deal.

Mr Harold Soref, M.P. (Con)
House of Commons

14 APRIL 1971

WHY THE TRAIN WAS LATE IN STARTING

SIR – On April 5 you reported that the 01.25 train from Paddington to South Wales did not depart from Paddington until 02.08 'due to the driver refusing three locomotives'.

I can assure you, sir, that the driver concerned is said to be considered by management as being a most conscientious person and did not at any time refuse locomotives as stated. The train was late departing from Paddington owing to the operational staff being unable to provide a suitable locomotive in fit mechanical condition to run the train on time. When a locomotive was produced at 01.40 the train finally departed from Paddington at 02.08.

Unfortunately this locomotive broke down at Reading owing to an empty engine radiator, and the train was further delayed. How do I know this? Because, sir, I was the driver concerned.

I am a regular reader of *The Daily Telegraph* and consider that what you do print is fairly reliable. I can only assume that some deskbound clerk on Western Region supplied you with wrong information.

Reg Townsend
Engineman
London, NW10

A spokesman for Western Region said: 'The delay was due to the driver refusing three locomotives because in his opinion they were not mechanically sound. He was quite entitled to do so.'

26 APRIL 1971

SIR – When reading the letter from engineman Mr Reg Townsend (April 14), one's mind boggled at the necessity for his rejection of three diesel locomotives before moving the train, and the subsequent failure of the fourth.

Such an occurrence would have been unheard of in Great Western days, but then, of course, the South Wales train would almost certainly have been headed by a beautiful 'Castle', and she would not have let her driver down at Reading or anywhere else on the road.

William G. Barber
Sandwich, Kent

9 AUGUST 1971
JOURNEYS BY TRAIN

SIR – The trouble with British Rail is that it is such a curate's egg. I have travelled from Grantham to Edinburgh and enjoyed the journey: the coaches were comfortable and attractive, and lunch was excellent. Yet recently I experienced the opposite. I went from Bournemouth to Nottingham, on a train which was filthy and without either restaurant or buffet.

When I complained I received an apology, hardly sufficient recompense for a wretched journey, and an explanation that there had not been time to clean the train. My reaction has been, together with other reasons, to buy a car.

J.M. Mather
Holy Trinity Vicarage
Ilkeston, Derbyshire

18 APRIL 1972
SHOWDOWN

SIR – As one of countless commuters affected by the railways go-slow, may I make two points?

First, I believe that the vast majority of commuters are as determined as I am that the railway unions' exorbitant demands should not be met, whatever the inconvenience to us. Secondly, I am confident that if the trains become impossible we will find other ways of travelling to and from our work.

This helps to harden my resolve that the current issue must be the showdown between democratic government and industrial anarchy.

Geoffrey Sayer
Coldwaltham, Sussex

19 APRIL 1972
RITUAL OF PAY NEGOTIATIONS

SIR – Do we have to go through this absurd and infuriating ritual ballet every year with every trade union?

It is called pay negotiation. The trade union puts in an inflated claim it knows will be refused. The employers – who, as likely as not, are losing money – make a counter-offer which, of course, is spurned. Perhaps a Government conciliator is brought in, and then finally, if the union graciously agrees – an arbitrator is appointed.

These ritual antics have been performed in the case of the railways. This time the arbitrator has given what amounts to an instant decision which – to no one's surprise – has as usual split the difference. Union rejection has ensued, but the Secretary for Employment has described it as a fair award.

(If fair, why was an unfair offer made earlier?)

I am not one who thinks that the 'national interest' should prevent doctors, nurses, power-station workers, miners, postmen, dustmen and railway employees from getting a fair wage. Whether one likes it or not this is not an authoritarian State. A trade union's job is primarily to get more money for its members and the employer's job is to make its organisation financially viable — or, at least, to minimise its losses.

The present dispute involves a straight fight over money. No one is forced to be an engine-driver, although everyone is supposed to want to be one. The Government, directly or indirectly, is an employer and should not be able to pass the buck. It should discuss and negotiate but ultimately come to a decision and be prepared to fight, although our welfare payments might have been specifically designed to help the striker and disrupter.

The people — the owners of the railways — should fight, no matter what it costs. Let us have another general strike if necessary. This annual Danegeld can be stopped only by an all-out fight on a just issue. The people are sick and tired of rising costs and are ready for a once-for-all confrontation with the unions. Let us have it now.

John Scott-Taggart
Beaconsfield, Bucks.

SIR — What redress is there for those of us who, having paid for season tickets on British Rail, because of the present chaos must drive to the nearest Tube station and pay once again for the privilege of getting to work at all?

F.J. Berthelsen
Kingston-upon-Thames

SPEEDY GO-SLOW

SIR – Having suffered British Rail's inefficiency for so long, I find it staggering that they are capable of organising a go-slow so quickly and with such effect. Surely there is some conclusion to be drawn from this?

(Mrs) M.M. Ford
London, WII

25 APRIL 1972

SIR – There hasn't been much to laugh at during the past week or so, as weary commuters and other rail travellers will testify. But a slight giggle was surely provided by Mr Buckton, locomen's general secretary, who, when required on Thursday under due process of law to suspend the operation of spite and malice, was reported to have said it was 'a sorry day for democracy'.

Mr Buckton's tongue may or may not have been in his cheek, but there was certainly plenty of cheek on his tongue.

Maxwell Wise
Kingsley Green, Surrey

24 MAY 1972

SIR – Permit me, please, as a retired rank and file railway - man, to urge railwaymen of all grades to vote against further industrial action in their industry. I 'answered the call' of the Railway Clerks' Association (now Transport Salaried Staffs Association) in 1926 and came out on strike to support the miners.

The result of this strike so far as the railways were concerned was catastrophic. We gave road transport a tremendous boost; we destroyed the confidence of our customers and lost business that was never regained; we so reduced the funds of the RCA that there had to be a levy of £1 per member to rebuild the union finances.

The labour troubles on the railways since 1926 have made it still more difficult to persuade traders and passengers to use rail services, and this has created and still is creating redundancies.

As a pensioner (but still with railway loyalties) I regard the increases in wages now offered as generous, and only wish such generosity prevailed prior to my retirement in 1969.

C.R. Williams
London, N10

26 FEBRUARY 1973
LIVING GIANTS

SIR – Whatever the advantages of Hovertrain or linear motor rail travel are supposed to be, neither can replace or even equal the power-beauty concept of the lost heart of railway travel, namely the steam locomotive.

Your photographer is to be congratulated on the fine shot of the *Flying Scotsman*, taken under dismal lighting conditions. Nobody who has stood on a railway platform when one of these living giants has belted through with a long train will ever forget the experience.

In the context of life-spice, interest and variety generally, I sometimes wonder whether we really are experiencing

progress or merely 'change'. The latter is not always necessarily the former.

Henry Bimpson
Liverpool

8 APRIL 1975
FIRST CLASS

SIR – Over the Easter holiday, travelling from Paddington to
Devon, my sister and I although travelling on second-class
tickets were lucky enough to be seated in a first-class carriage
which was specially marked for the use of second-class
passengers.

The extra comfort found in those deeply plushy seats was
at once obvious, and our journey was comfortable and
warm.

In these days when it seems to be the 'in' thing to snipe at
so-called privilege we wondered how much longer the railway
unions would allow their workers to tolerate first-class
passengers. Surely there is very little difference in the
passenger paying for extra comfort and the patient of a
private hospital or nursing home doing the same?

Benita Brown
London, W5

8 JANUARY 1976
BENT DOUBLE

SIR – I hate to complain about dear old British Rail – but
they really do stick their neck out!

Having charged me £20 to travel first-class from
Huntingdon to Bristol they provided me with a plastic

spoon with which to stir my paper cup of coffee. Evidently the spoon was very embarrassed as, immediately I applied it, it bent itself into a complete circle and disappeared below the surface.

Robert E. Huband
Graveley, Cambs.

11 FEBRUARY 1976
RAILWAY LINES

SIR – In all the current discussion about closure of railway lines the only consideration seems to be the continued employment of staff. Has nobody a thought for the thousands of people who still need railway transport?

E. St A. Brooksbank
Epsom, Surrey

26 APRIL 1976
RAILWAY PROFIT

SIR – I hope that those in authority at British Railways gave their most profound consideration to your report (April 21) that the Bluebell Railway, five miles of single track in Sussex, *made a profit of £10,000 last year*.

Jean Lyell
London, SW3

29 APRIL 1976

SIR – Every year the Bluebell Railway in Sussex produces a creditable profit (Mrs Jean Lyell, April 26). And every year someone writes to the newspapers holding this up as an example to the managers of British Rail.

Without detracting from the success of the Bluebell boys, it really is time your readers were told that British Rail – and *The Daily Telegraph* – could make a profit if they, too, relied largely on volunteer, unpaid labour.

Eric Merrill
British Railways Board
London, NWI

16 FEBRUARY 1977
ROAD AND RAIL

SIR – In your newspaper (Feb. 9) there is a report 'Buses may replace loss-making trains', which tells us that the National Union of Railwaymen has agreed to consider a British Rail proposal to replace loss-making passenger branch services with buses following similar routes.

Shades of Beeching when almost identical promises were made, and hardly ever honoured!

The report goes on to expound that 'basically what is proposed is a partial interchange of roles between rail and road passenger transport. Inter-City rail service would provide *all* long-distance public passenger transport between main centres of population and express coach services would be *restricted* to routes on which they did not compete with rail services.'

The report goes on to visualise categories indicating in no uncertain terms that this integration of road and rail is in effect to limit and deny the choice of the ordinary individual *to choose his mode of travel*.

If this proposal comes into being for travel by rail only between main centres of population, with the blessing of the

NUR, who undoubtedly have in mind a monopoly and consequent wage negotiations, shall we then be faced with passenger fares so high, as all competition will have been eliminated, that trains on these routes will be empty and cut for lack of use, with further deterioration of our railways?

This fills me with foreboding and the fear that 1984 is almost with us.

Thomas L. Dimond
London, SW20

4 MAY 1977
TAKING COMFORT OUT OF TRAVEL

SIR – Your report on British Rail's plans for better passenger services omits to mention the ingenuity and diligence which British Rail design 'experts' have devoted to making the interiors of main-line passenger coaches more and more uncomfortable.

The compartment, which used to ensure seclusion, has been abolished in favour of open coaches where the seated passenger may be ceaselessly disturbed by the marching up and down the centre aisle of the restless.

The old deeply upholstered first-class comfort has been abolished in favour of unyielding seats no better than those of a bus, and which after an hour or so produce creeping paralysis of the hinder parts.

With a particularly brilliant stroke of design, these seats have been provided with hard armrests with rectangular edges, and are upholstered in shiny plastic; the passenger's elbow and his suit may thus be attacked simultaneously.

The window sills of these air-conditioned coaches are so high that a person of middling height feels claustrophobic and the shorter can barely see over at all. By a further imaginative stroke, there are no exclusively smoking and no-smoking coaches, but each is half and half, though without partition and a closing door between. The result is that, notwithstanding the expensive air-conditioning system, a stale tang of fag smoke can be detected in all no-smoking sections. Non-smokers should therefore be warned that for practical purposes there are no smoke-free zones on British Rail Inter-City services.

To garnish the physical discomfort of these new coaches, the decor is of a garish orange upholstery, porridge plastic walls and ceiling, and vividly striped carpets; and the lighting is largely supplied by glaring fluorescent strip-units in the ceiling.

Nor is this all. Many of the lavatory door latches do not latch. You can no longer wash in a basin of hot water but only beneath a hand spray; a feature unknown in any comfortable hotel, club or home. The lavatories are so cramped that large persons should take care lest they get wedged between the apparatus, the door and the window. The train catering is now reduced to chips-with-everything grills: the standard squalor of British mass-catering.

When one considers the traditional comforts of rail travel still to be seen in railway museums, it seems clear that common sense has been vanquished at British Rail by the expert's ergonomic and interior design, and that he has superbly matched the achievements of his brother experts in the fields of town planning and housing.

Correlli Barnett
Churchill College, Cambridge

7 MAY 1977

SIR – Mr Correlli Barnett needs to experience the conditions on some of the European trains – he would then cease to complain about British Rail.

In a first-class sleeper from the Hook of Holland to Berlin the sheets on the bed were grey and damp, there was no heat in the carriage and only a trickle of rusty cold water in the basin, from which the stench was unbelievable.

There was no refreshment of any kind on the train – not even drinking water.

On the overnight journey from Stockholm to Copenhagen the first-class sleeper was old and shabby and had never been anything but strictly utility. On the last part of this particular journey on my way home a so-called restaurant car was put on the train at Hengelo in Holland, and I can only describe the plate of food served to me as revolting and every single utensil was plastic.

However I strongly recommend breakfast on the Hook Continental from Harwich to Liverpool Street. Even if the bill makes you wince, it is worth every penny and you feel specially glad to be home.

Francis Howard-Gwynne
London, SW16

SIR – I was most interested to read the letter from Mr Correlli Barnett concerning comfort on British Rail coaches. I most heartily agree with his comments but would emphasise that he left out the most unkind cut of all, *i.e.* that given to the lower region of your body as you try and get in or out from under that blasted table.

Richard Sharman
Shaldon, Devon

SIR – Commenting on the difficulties of modern railway coaches listed by Mr Correlli Barnett (May 4), may I express surprise, even despair, that British Railways design experts are so unwilling to learn from their colleagues in the Common Market?

In French main-line trains seats are comfortable and served with well-directed overhead spot lamps, passenger-controlled, as in aircraft. Before each seat a firm and flat folding table is well placed. Air conditioning is excellent; sills and folding arm rests convenient.

Immediately on starting (punctually) the greetings and good wishes from the conductor, gently conveyed over loudspeakers, provide a friendly welcome, and this address system is used to provide announcements a few minutes before forthcoming stops. It is, I understand, also used to give news of reasons for any unanticipated stops or slight delays.

Furthermore the coaches are quiet and run smoothly at all speeds. And the trains arrive on time (except when there is a strike of course!).

When will the British learn?

Brian A. Mead
Bournemouth

SIR – I am amazed at Mr Correlli Barnett's criticism of the new main-line coaches introduced by British Rail. I travel extensively by BR (much preferable to a private car) and I find these coaches comfortable, relaxing and free from the claustrophobic and dusty atmosphere of older types, far easier to work in, and although only of middling heigh' myself I can see out of the windows perfectly well.

High time we stopped beating BR with ill-dire

complaints. On the whole long-distance rail travel has improved very significantly in recent years, and the only pity is that we can't afford to use it more often for pleasure. Even so, away-day schemes and their like offer excellent value. A little more encouragement for trying, please!

D.H. Barnard
Kidlington, Oxon.

10 MAY 1977

SIR — In his letter about rail travel comfort Mr Correlli Barnett (May 4) laments the fact that British Rail's new Inter-City coaches are open saloons. Your readers may be interested to know that over the period during which open saloons have replaced compartment coaches business on Inter-City routes has grown by nearly 50 per cent, and it is still growing.

We believe this is due to the overall improvement in the quality of service to which the new coaches have made a significant contribution. But whatever the reason, the growth is a clear indication that we are pursuing a policy that is meeting a demand.

P.A. Keen
Chief Passenger Manager, British Railways Board
London, NW1

12 MAY 1977

SIR – Mr Brian A. Mead's experience of French railways (May 7) must certainly have been totally different from mine. While British Rail obviously have their faults, the SNCF are considerably worse.

On the route from Paris to Orleans the trains have seats that are far from comfortable since the backs are too upright and the upholstery made from plastic which becomes extremely sticky in hot weather.

I have certainly never seen any of the luxuries that Mr Mead mentions such as spot-lamps, tables or air-conditioning. Wind-down windows, filthy ashtrays and little curtains which obstruct the view are the only concessions to passenger comfort. Moreover I have never heard greetings from the staff of the train and in my experience their time-keeping is at least as poor as that of British Rail.

The coaches suffer from being very dirty. Passengers suffer from earache if they sit in the corner seats where there is an ear-shattering noise of compressed air at every halt. French trains are not my idea of travelling in comfort especially when there are not enough coaches provided, as on the connection route from Boulogne to Paris, and sitting on a suitcase in the gangway is necessary. The difference in quality of travel on either side of the Channel is most marked.

While British Rail may have its irregularities it is certainly preferable to riding in a cattle truck.

Peter Lloyd
Stanmore, Middlesex

NOWHERE TO SIT

SIR – The letter from Mr Correlli Barnett (May 4) calls attention to many of the more obscure and subtle ways that British Rail has adopted to discourage passenger traffic – ways which have undoubtedly cost them a good deal of money in outside designers' fees to achieve.

It is only fair to point out, however, that they have also used more direct, brutal and cheaper methods such as the almost complete removal of seats (which used to exist) in practically all places where passengers have to wait for trains.

This applies particularly to main stations where most waiting is done. A prime example is Lime Street, Liverpool, where there are *no* seats at all in the concourse and no, repeat, *no*, waiting-room except one exclusively for females.

Elderly males (of which I am one), however infirm, must stand or squat (if they can) for the hours which they may have to wait.

When I complained to an official about this it was justified by the remark that this was 'the modern trend'.

C.S.L. Incledon
Willersey, Glos.

23 MAY 1977
DISCOMFORT ON BRITISH RAILWAYS

SIR – The letter from Mr P.A. Keen, Chief Passenger Manager, British Railways Board (May 10) entirely fulfilled my expectations, being the customary British Rail refusal to answer, let alone act upon, the criticisms offered by the hapless passengers they 'manage'.

Did British Rail conduct a poll of passengers as to their

preference between open saloons and compartments before abolishing the compartment? Or was the decision an arbitrary one based on the railways' own technical and operating convenience? Would it not have been possible at least to have constructed a proportion of compartment coaches so that passengers could enjoy a choice? Is it not an observable fact that the 'non-smoking' sections of the open coaches smell of fag-smoke? And why are there not exclusively non-smoking coaches instead of all half-and-half? Is it not also true (as the photographs in British Rail's own advertisements prove) that the sills of windows are nearer shoulder than elbow height – and that this is not the case in the latest European stock?

Do the armchairs in Mr Keen's own sitting-room at home in any way resemble the latest British Rail seats in terms of shape and upholstery? And would he care to have his own sitting-room or dining-room decorated in porridge, tangerine and black?

Perhaps Mr Keen will be kind enough to give us straight answers to these questions, rather than again take refuge, by his own admission, in such a blatant *non sequitur* as arguing that because Inter-City traffic has gone up 50 per cent in the period since open saloons replaced compartments, this must prove that British Rail are providing the kind of comfort the public wants.

Could it not be that the public likes the faster times and more frequent services resulting from electrification and more powerful diesels? But why should one not be drawn at such high speeds in the same standard of interior comfort as used to distinguish our railways?

Correlli Barnett
Churchill College, Cambridge

3 JUNE 1977

SIR – When I replied to Mr Correlli Barnett's criticism of our use of open saloon-type stock by saying that we believe that the new coaches had made a significant contribution to the 50 per cent growth of business on Inter-City routes, I hoped that he would accept my short-hand and give us credit for founding our beliefs on some evidence. Alas, I have merely fulfilled his low expectations of British Rail.

To meet Mr Barnett's points in detail, sir, takes rather more space. I hope you will forgive me – *non mea culpa*.

Firstly we have researched public attitudes on the 'open versus compartment' question not once but a number of times. We have found that what started as a neutral acceptance of open stock has gradually developed into a positive preference for it; not, of course, by everyone, but by the majority of travellers. Mr Barnett is one of a distinguished but diminishing minority.

The decision to standardise on opens *does* have technical and operational advantages. Taking all the factors together, we have better economics – which benefit the passenger and the taxpayer alike, though they expose me to the slings and arrows of Mr Barnett!

Next we prefer to make coaches totally 'smoking' or 'non-smoking' if possible. But sometimes this gets the 'mix' of accommodation wrong and we have to divide coaches. We have only had 'smoke drift' in one design and we are putting that right.

The sills of carriage windows are higher than they used to be. Our medical advisers told us it reduced eye strain. Personally, I was sceptical, but now I am convinced.

It must be a matter of pure coincidence that my home

décor includes Mr Barnett's hated 'porridge, tangerine and black' for no one consulted me on these matters of personal taste. I was not in the job at the time. We have had a good feedback on using bright colours rather than dull ones. The shape of our armchairs does point a moral, however. Being lazy, I slump in a 'comfortable' chair and get curvature of the spine. My wife, in a chair which induces a better posture, is more comfortable in the long run.

And it's the long run that British Rail is interested in – but with High Speed Trains it's getting shorter all the time.

Really I'm beginning to enjoy this correspondence, but perhaps you, sir, would prefer that we continued it elsewhere.

Peter Keen
Chief Passenger Manager, British Railways Board
London, NW1

18 JULY 1978
RAILWAY SMOKERS

SIR – As only 40 per cent of the people are estimated to be smokers I wonder why the ratio of non-smoking carriages to smoking carriages on British Rail is still approximately 50-50?

Even if 40 per cent of the population does smoke, my experience as a British Rail commuter suggests that this is not the ratio for British Rail passengers. This morning I had to take a seat in a smoking carriage (because the non-smoking seats were all taken) and only 10 to 20 per cent of the people there smoked. The ratio of smoking to non-smoking compartments on the tube seems more realistic, being about 25 per cent.

I cannot understand why British Rail does not conduct a small census among the passengers and take appropriate action.

M.H. Sibson
Brasted, Kent

22 JULY 1978

SIR – The ratio of smoking to non-smoking carriages (Mr M.H. Sibson's letter July 18) has been researched on a more scientific (albeit local) basis.

Following marked deterioration of service last year on the Waterloo–Portsmouth line, the Haslemere and Witley Rail Users Action Group carried out a detailed survey of regular travellers in early December 1977 and received over 600 completed questionnaires.

In response to one of the 17 questions which were posed: 'Do you prefer to travel in smoking or non-smoking accommodation?' 79.4 per cent wished to travel in non-smoking accommodation.

Since the ratio seems to be about 50-50 in practice this means that almost 30 per cent of rail users may have to travel in conditions which do not suit them.

Peter M. Smith
Haslemere, Surrey

29 JULY 1978

SIR – May I assure Mr M.H. Sibson (July 18) that British Rail is fully aware of the growing number of non-smokers among its passengers, and will be increasing the proportion of no-smoking accommodation to meet their needs, although with a fleet of some 17,000 coaches, these changes will take time to complete.

The precise level will necessarily vary between differing types of trains – simply because of the varied interior layouts of our coaches – but on the Southern Region services on which Mr Sibson commutes we are aiming for 67–75 per cent non-smoking accommodation.

P.A. Keen
Chief Passenger Manager, British Railways Board
London, NW1

THE GUM CHEWERS

SIR – Mr P.M. Smith's argument (July 22) is fallacious.

A non-smoker may use a smoking compartment but a smoker may not use a non-smoking compartment. Thus if 70 per cent prefer non-smoking and there are 30 per cent of smokers, a 50-50 ration of compartments would seem to be about right.

Incidentally, will he next ask about chewing gum or eating sandwiches, habits some people find as obnoxious as smoking?

(Dr) S.L. Henderson-Smith
Huddersfield

4 AUGUST 1978

SIR – Dr S.L. Henderson-Smith's rhetorical question (July 29) is quite illogical.

Smoking is obnoxious to non-smokers because of the physical discomfort it causes them. How can he say the same of gum chewers or sandwich eaters?

Eating one's sandwiches on a train may be an economic necessity or, indeed, a starvation remedy, as on some long distance trains, e.g., a Balkan express on which I recently travelled when, for many hours, buffet or restaurant cars were not attached.

Dr A. Campbell Reid F.R.C.S.
Sheffield

SIR – It is Dr S.L. Henderson-Smith's argument (July 29) that is fallacious.

To avoid offensive and injurious fumes a non-smoker must use a non-smoking compartment. A smoker may use any part of the train – all he has to do is refrain from smoking.

(Dr) P.T. Gilbert
Ilkley, Yorks.

21 JULY 1978
JOBS FOR THE BOYS?

SIR – It seems that 15-year-old schoolboys find little difficulty in driving British Rail's latest locomotives (your report July 19).

One wonders what this will do to the standing of ASLEF members, always so quick to point out the high degrees of skill necessary to drive modern trains.

With continuing calls for double manning by ASLEF, British Rail might like to consider recruiting some 15-year-old schoolboys instead.

M.R. Houghton
Devizes, Wilts.

28 JULY 1978

RAILWAY SKILLS

SIR – I find M.R. Houghton's view of 'skill' ('Jobs for the boys', July 21) particularly naive. Sir Richard Marsh, former Chairman of British Rail, once observed that there are '27 million railway experts and 190,000 of us who earn our living on the railway'. Clearly things have not changed.

Mr Houghton suggests that the ease with which three boys drove away two British Rail locomotives completely undermines the Associated Society of Locomotive Engineers and Firemen's claims that a driver's job is one that demands great skill. I would remind this gentleman that the minimum period of qualification from secondman to driver is at least 385 turns of duty – about two-and-a-half years. In practice this period is often longer. This is because the skill needed to 'drive trains' is the skill of experience. It is extremely unlikely that Mr Houghton will ever face the horror of trying to stop 1070 metric tons in 600 metres because a child of five is playing on the railway track. Or, less dramatically, that he will have to cope with faulty signalling or the complexities of modern locomotive electronics.

If Mr Houghton believes a driver's job to be easy, I suggest he joins British Rail as a traction trainee and stops casting aspersions on the nature of a particularly demanding job.

M.M. Christelow
Projects Manager, Inter-City Railway Soc.
Bedale, Yorks.

19 JULY 1979
COSTLY DISTINCTION

SIR — My wife and I recently travelled from Euston to Coventry on the Inter-City express: the train was crowded, but we managed to secure the last two seats. On our way to these we passed three practically empty first-class coaches: on the return journey the situation was similar.

I appreciate that in the days of wooden benches and parliament-enforced cheap travel these distinctions were necessary, but does this still apply in 1979? The fuel expended alone in pushing this near-empty rolling stock about the country must outweigh the trifling increase in revenue.

F.N. Scaife
Portsmouth

21 JULY 1979
STEAM'S LAST LAUGH

SIR — I note that the planning application for the Bluebell Railway's extension to East Grinstead has been turned down.

The shades of Ruskin and Wordsworth must have been supporting dwellers alongside the proposed line in their opposition to the scheme. Is it not strange how the arguments against the coming of the railway, 150 years ago, live on in our council chambers?

One marvels at the inevitability of new roads, with new earthworks and destruction of property, all at public expense, yet a private railway, seeking to make use of an existing formation at private expense is suppressed when at all possible.

When the oil in the world is burnt the steam train will have the last laugh of all.

T. Stewart Jephcote
Blandford Forum, Dorset

15 JANUARY 1980
STANDING IN COMFORT

SIR – The sum of £26 million seems to be a lot to ensure that 'people will be able to stand in comfort' on suburban trains (your report, Jan. 9).

However, while standing they will be able to look through the windows, a feat which is impossible from any seat. If London Transport can design a sliding-door train with all-round passenger visibility, why cannot British Railways?

E.C. Dawes
New Malden, Surrey

15 FEBRUARY 1980
IT'S ALL OUR FAULT

SIR – I have long suspected that British Rail thinks it could run an efficient service if it was not for the inconvenience of having to convey people.

This opinion was strengthened recently when I heard the announcer at Cannon Street say at the end of a stumbling apology for a late arrival on platform 1, '. . . and we apologise for any inconvenience caused by passengers'.

N.J. Milliner
Sevenoaks, Kent

13 AUGUST 1980

HIGH-SPEED DISCOMFORT

SIR — The '125' high-speed trains on the Paddington line have developed a characteristic.

As they enter a tunnel at speed air pressure affects the ears in a similar way to air travel. One should swallow or yawn to normalise the effect and repeat the process at the end of the tunnel.

Is it peculiar to this route or is it common to 125s in tunnels in other areas?

Mervyn Madge
Plymouth

19 AUGUST 1980

SIR — The pressure pulses experienced by Mr Mervyn Madge (Aug. 13) when high-speed trains pass through tunnels have been well known to British Rail for many years.

They are currently sponsoring an intensive research programme at Dundee University to compare various ways of alleviating the problem.

Previous research contracts have been awarded to me and to other investigators at several universities, notably Cambridge, Leeds and Liverpool.

Early work on this topic was carried out in the 1930s, but little progress was made until the early 1960s when the Japanese began to develop the Shin-Kansen network.

Within the past 15 years or so, most of the research effort has been undertaken in Britain and much of this has been financed by British Rail. We now know that the 'ear-popping' sensation can be alleviated in various ways involving modifications to tunnels or trains.

The variety of responses of different individuals to sudden pressure fluctuations is remarkable. If Mr Madge observes his fellow passengers, he will find that many do not react at all to the pressure changes that he experiences.

A few people with severe colds might find exceptionally large fluctuations quite uncomfortable, but no one will be subjected to pain, and there is certainly no question of damaging the ears.

Prof. A.E. Vardy
University of Dundee

23 AUGUST 1980

SIR – I am unable to agree with Prof A.E. Vardy's statement (Aug 19) that ear popping will not damage the ears.

Many years ago I was driving an electric train; the front of the cab, being flat, hit the air under a low bridge at 70 m.p.h. compressing the air and causing what I can only describe as hissing in my left ear, and the noise has never ceased.

W.E. Woodward
Frinton-on-Sea, Essex

4 DECEMBER 1980
TIME BR WAS GIVEN CREDIT

SIR – Mr Ian Waller's examination of British Rail's economics (article, Dec. 1) is intelligent and constructive. The same cannot be said for your leader of the same date.

You admit that many European railways are more heavily

subsidised than our own; yet you are opposed to increasing Government expenditure on British Rail. You then make the amazing claim that 'other countries seem to get better value for the money that goes into their railways'.

Is this really true? I think not. No other European country operates a frequent service of 125 m.p.h. trains, available to both first- and second-class fare payers and without supplementary charges. Nowhere else in Europe is there an equivalent of the advanced passenger train, able to run at 125 m.p.h. on existing tracks and to shorten journey times by tilting on curves. This is British technology and technology of which we should be proud.

No other European city has such a vast influx of commuters as has London – with the associated expense of track, trains and men provided for only three hours each day. And only in Britain, it seems, does the railway system suffer from a predominantly hostile Tory Press which cannot forget the nationalisation after the war.

It is not British Rail but successive Governments which have created an economic crisis of almost unprecedented severity. Naturally this has adversely affected BR's carryings. It is up to the Government to recompense British Rail – adequately – and to accept fully the blame for any reductions in service which result from its failure to invest sensibly in the railway system.

C. Hobley
London, W5

TIME FOR THEIR MONEY

SIR – On the first day of the increase in fares, British Rail accorded travellers on the 07.38 Billingshurst to Victoria the privilege of 22 minutes extra travelling time. On the return journey it was an extra 23 minutes.

Nobody can doubt that this is value for money! Well done Sir Peter Parker, for an 18 per cent rise in fares, a 30 per cent increase in travelling time!

J.M. Chick
Billingshurst, Sussex

POLICY LIKE A RAILWAY SANDWICH

SIR – Your leader headed 'Running a Railway', curls up as dry and unappetising as any proverbial British Rail cheese sandwich, the more so since it appeared alongside Mr Ian Waller's fresh and realistic analysis of the State network's problems.

The problem facing the railway system is not, as you postulated, the question of whether to send more subsidies chasing after an operating deficit, but to *invest* in new equipment, particularly electrification, required to provide a network capable of giving more value for money. That we should return to another era of Beeching cuts and possible 'Orpington' revolts by distressed commuters will simply trim even further the railways' chance of survival.

As Mr Waller points out, but your leader does not, we already have a good railway, in European terms, in pure cost-benefit terms. Every other European nation, mindful of the energy crisis, is investing heavily in railways and particularly in improving commuter services.

Paris is an excellent example but many quite small German cities possess transport systems, attractive and heavily used, which put Britain to shame.

A decision now virtually to abandon the railways will have disastrous economic consequences for the future of this country in an age where there will be no certainties concerning the supply and use of energy resources.

Richard Cottrell
Member European Parliament
Wells, Somerset

MOBILITY OF LABOUR

SIR – Why not extend the £1 old age pensioner concessionary rail fare to the unemployed, so that they can get around and look?

Basil Tudor
London, N1

6 DECEMBER 1980
CONGRATULATIONS TO TRAIN GUARD

SIR – In answer to the question posed by Mr Ian Waller (article, Dec. 1), 'Any hope for the commuter?' I would venture the reply:

'Only if he has the patience of Job and an extraordinarily good sense of humour.' For without both of these attributes he will surely be tearing his hair out by the end of his journey, overcome by anger and frustration!

Every week I travel 240 miles by train between Buxton and Manchester at a weekly cost of £16.90. Delays and can-cellations are so commonplace that on the infrequent occasions when the train actually departs and arrives on time one can scarcely control one's delight and resist the urge to slap the guard on the back with a hearty 'Congratulations!'

On one occasion I boarded the 5.15 p.m. from

Manchester and should have arrived in Buxton at 6.12 p.m. In fact the train crawled into Buxton at 7.20 p.m. when we were apologetically informed that three trains had broken down, including our own antiquated model.

'This is the age of the train,' says Jimmy Savile. In fact if we really knew the age of the trains still in service on some lines, we might be deterred from embarking on our journey in the first place and we might be even more indignant at the recent price increase.

Perhaps the commuter's best hope is to ensure when he sets out on his journey that he has a good book with him – how about *Murder on the Orient Express*?

T.M. Edge
Buxton, Derbyshire

GOOD BUSINESS IN MOSCOW

SIR – British Rail are to be congratulated upon its bold move which enables Railcard holders who are senior citizens to travel anywhere in a day for £1.

My wife and I have thus been able to visit friends who are physically unable to come and see us and it has cheered them up.

When we were in Moscow this year we were able to travel anywhere on their Metro (equivalent to the Tube in London) and the charge of 5 kopecs (about $3\frac{1}{2}$p) results in millions of people using the Metro every day.

Certain industries and services can make a success with low charges whereas by continually increasing charges demand will fall and result in financial failure.

A. Reuben Wilson
Bournemouth

UNGUARDED MOMENT

SIR — Long-suffering passengers on the Western Region's Waterloo to Exeter St David's line have long become conditioned to the inefficiency of British Rail — mishaps include running out of diesel fuel, innumerable engine breakdowns including fires, a carriage door falling off and even the driver failing to stop at a scheduled station.

However, on the 7.10 p.m. from Waterloo on Nov. 28, passengers' cool was severely tested when, on making the usual routine stop at Tisbury, the guard managed to get left behind.

What on earth will happen next?

O.A. Burge
London, SW7

A GREEN LOOK

SIR — Mr C. Hobley (Dec. 4) gives fair dues. But not quite. Many BR services are excellent; others merit varying degrees of criticism.

Has Mr Hobley not heard of the Japanese high-speed trains? Or of multiple voltage and dual-gauge TEEs that have operated in Europe for years, many with facilities we do not have? What is the use of travelling at 125 m.p.h. upright on curves only to be sick *en route* and to arrive looking green?

I rather like the overnight sleepers, especially to Inverness; old-fashioned perhaps, except in speed. Excellent courtesy on the stations generally from half a mile north of Watford. And the cheapest sleepers in Europe to boot.

Lest Sir Peter Parker be tempted, they are also not the best. But pretty good.

T. Brentini
London, NW6

TRANSPORT OF DELIGHT

SIR – I had not realised, until I was waiting for a railway connection at Doncaster last week, that the old-fashioned hobby of train spotting is still with us in these modern high-speed days, when three boys in the waiting room dashed from side to side logging the passing trains.

This compulsive notching-up of numbers always seemed to me to be a curious occupation, particularly when the young son of a friend persuaded his grandmother to cover Paddington one day, while he did Euston.

This lady is, in fact, the only female I have heard of to engage in this young masculine pursuit.

L.R. Sanders
London, NW3

RAIL: BEST TRANSPORT FOR THE FUTURE

SIR – It was with amazement that I read your leader 'Can We Afford Railways?' (April 20). It disheartens me to read yet another attack on our railway system, even more so when we should surely be trying to support all forms of transport (and here I include the often forgotten waterways) as much as possible.

It is true that British Rail receives a subsidy from the Government. However, this covers passenger services only and not rail freight, which is entirely self-financing. Might I also point out that BR's passenger subsidy is, with the exception of Sweden, the lowest in Western Europe, and that BR's percentage of costs covered by revenues the highest of any railway in Europe. British Rail is not some 'relic of the 19th century', but a modern, efficient transportation system.

Where the Government has invested in special rail projects – and there is a difference between investment and subsidy – then British Rail has been spectacularly successful, with such services as the High Speed Trains being widely acknowledged as the best of their kind in Europe, if not the world.

Surely Britain's future transport systems will rely more on a fast, electrified rail network which would be more efficient and less damaging to the environment than an already overcrowded motorway system.

P.J. Simpson
Burton-on-Trent, Staffs.

EXPENSIVE LUXURY

SIR – Your leader on the need to convert railways into roads was surely more suited to April 1 than April 20!

Does not train travel cost something like 7 pence a mile, and car travel more like 20 pence a mile? Add to that the unrecognised but real cost of road transport – of air pollution, noise pollution, vibration damage and collision damage, to say nothing of road injuries and deaths (incalculable).

I run a car myself, and appreciate its advantages. I also appreciate that in more senses than one it is an expensive luxury, and that as a social necessity we need to be able to travel by rail whenever possible.

Michael Wilcock
Bristol

28 APRIL 1981
COSTS OF RUNNING A RAILWAY

SIR — I was delighted to see that your little Bank Holiday leader advocating turning railways into roads was effectively challenged within 48 hours.

The challenge came from your own Transport Correspondent who wrote on April 22 that it was not realistic to think that the 400,000 people who daily commute by train to London could be switched to road transport without causing chaos, and that the cost of converting railways into roads would also be more expensive than that of modernising the train services.

It is not surprising that you were confused over costs, as you describe the proposal to spend £775 million over 20 years on further main-line electrification of BR as 'a *multi-billion* electrification programme which sober analysts put at three times Sir Peter Parker's estimates'.

Who are these sober analysts? Are they more sober than the joint team from the Department of Transport and BR, who studied the issue for some two-and-a-half years, with input from other Government departments and a wide range of outside bodies?

Sir Peter Parker
Chairman, British Railways Board
London, NW1

SIR – If only Karl Benz had preceded George Stephenson the railways would never have been built and would not now be such a huge burden on our economy.

Even today your leader of April 20 suggesting that we should cut our losses on the railways and convert them to roads will go unheeded. The alliance between the rail unions and the followers of the Rev. W. Awdry supported by BR's tax-financed advertising will prove too powerful. The losses will clearly have to pile up much higher yet before good sense prevails.

You print two predictable replies (April 24). Mr P.J. Simpson tells us that BR's losses are the lowest of any country in Europe. Surely this only proves that no railway can operate at prices its customers are freely prepared to pay?

Mr Michael Wilcock says how cheap rail travel is at only 7p per mile compared with 20 by car. His train price seems to be based only on very long journeys, the fare per mile being higher on shorter trips.

It also takes no account of the price paid through taxes or of the wasted distance travelled on most train journeys to and from the stations at each end.

M.D. Noar
Hollingbourne, Kent

30 APRIL 1981

RAILWAYS PASS THE TEST OF BAD WEATHER

SIR – Today, April 26, the radio says the M4 is blocked by snow, the M5 is just passable, all traffic in the West Midlands and Bristol is virtually at a standstill, and Wales and the West Country are similarly threatened. This after bad weather has closed most of the main roads in the North of England and Scotland for some days.

I did not hear that British Rail has not been able to run trains because of snow; no freight train jack-knifed and blocked the lines. Indeed the sensible way to travel in this weather is by BR.

Yet this is the system you would dismantle and throw away, according to your leader (April 20). I am disappointed and disgusted by this narrow outlook.

I support Mr P.J. Simpson and Mr Michael Wilcock (April 24) in saying that British Rail should be given all the investment possible. BR is as important to the country as is BL. I would hope that some of this investment could be devoted to an increasing effort to move freight off the roads on to the rails. It is a ludicrous situation that BR is closing its trans-Pennine freight line because of the losses incurred when trans-Pennine roads can become impassable because of bad weather.

British Rail's plans to electrify virtually all its present system can provide thousands of jobs for many years, it can conserve oil, and will provide a better return than any money spent on overcrowded motorways.

E.B. Stott
Pinner, Middlesex

STOP PLAYING TRAINS

SIR – Some readers evidently cannot bear to face the fact that railways are finished throughout the world.

This relic can be kept going for 50 years if we allow them to keep sucking our blood. More sensible, however, to turn them into roads for use exclusively by heavy transport lorries and coaches.

The improvement on existing roads would be enormous. The cost of conversion would be much less than new roads and they could be self-supporting by a charge on users. In fact they could be owned and maintained by the transport industry itself.

If and when petrol becomes uneconomic, the existing overhead wires could be used to supply electricity to vehicles fitted with trolleys in an update of the trolley buses. Science may even give us a new fuel by then.

But now is the time to stop playing trains.

A.L. Rogers
Walsall, W. Midlands

2 MAY 1981

CONTRAST IN TRANSPORT CASUALTIES

SIR – Not a single passenger was killed on British Railways last year compared with the daily death toll on our roads of about 20 people.

This fact alone should make us all bless the name of George Stephenson and wish that Karl Benz had never been born.

R.V. Banks
Chairman, Railway Development Soc.
Maidstone, Kent

5 MAY 1981

GIVING RAILWAYS CREDIT

SIR – There is a feeling around that *The Daily Telegraph* is increasingly becoming a rather comical survivor of an age that is plainly past – an age far removed from the overcrowded hurly-burly we find ourselves in today. After reading your recent leader, headed 'Can We Afford Railways?' one can understand why.

On principle, the idea of large-scale rail closures at a time when energy is patently becoming scarce and expensive (and the roads ever more of a deathtrap) is criminally selfish and short-sighted. It may feel like striking a blow for personal freedom and convenience – but at an enormous cost to future generations, who would have to re-convert. The days of such pipe dreams are over.

Be careful, sir, lest in your urge to denigrate and discredit the railways wherever possible you lose credibility yourself.

Lionel Scott
Weston Favell, Northants.

7 MAY 1981
RAILWAYS OF THE FUTURE

SIR – I have followed the correspondence on railways with great interest but feel that Mr A.L. Rogers's letter (April 30) summarises the arguments most succinctly.

His observations on what to do when diesel (not petrol, surely?) oil is no longer available for commercial road vehicles is most interesting. He suggests overhead electrification of the system and pantographs on the vehicles. All that will be necessary then to achieve maximum efficiency will be to fit flanged wheels to the vehicles and lay rails on the roadbed thus enabling large quantities of passengers and goods to be moved both quickly and safely.

Or is that where we began?

Richard J.P. Vokes
Pulham St Mary, Norfolk

21 AUGUST 1981
UNLUCKY NUMBER

SIR – On my last 14 journeys by rail – all in Scotland – the diesel locomotive has broken down on 13. Is this a record?

Nevile Reid
Kildary, Invergordon

29 AUGUST 1981

SIR – Mr Nevile Reid, doubtless, feels just cause to complain about diesel locomotive failure in Scotland (Aug. 21). In my recent holiday travel by rail I wasn't nearly so fortunate! Visiting Oban, Mallaig, Fort William, Inverness, Thurso, Perth, Kirkculdy, Edinburgh and Stirling involved my travelling through country of such majesty and beauty that I would have welcomed 100 locomotive breakdowns, especially to observe more closely the wild duck and the other birds which help to make Scotland an unforgettable experience.

J.L. Harris
Mountain Ash, Mid-Glamorgan

25 MARCH 1982
NO SMOKING IN BUFFET CARS

SIR – Apropos of the report by Mr Con Coughlin on March 22 concerning smoking in buffet cars I agree with the Freedom Organisation for the Right to Enjoy Smoking Tobacco. On the Victoria to Littlehampton train I asked regular travellers to sign their names.

I asked if they agreed with the statement: 'I am against the withdrawal of the smoking facility in buffet cars and do not wish to jeopardise the livelihood of stewards by such action.'

The 16 signatures I collected represent 289 years of travel and support for rail catering. We feel that the head of the stewards' trade union should take action to return the buffets to their former status. You cannot run a buffet car by selling cups of tea to school children.

Short-journey travellers might have a drink and a smoke before they board the train. We commuters of journeys taking two hours relax while on the move. We feel that it is about time minority monopolists are stopped from imposing restrictions.

If other buffet car regulars signed such a petition the amount of protesters would be several hundred-fold.

Peter C. Hart
and 15 others
London, SE1

SIR – We are told constantly that we should take the strain of travelling by using the train, for this is the age . . .

And then . . . Jimmy Savile encourages us to use the train, enjoy a cup of tea (instant) and we watch him sit back and smoke his cigar. He will not be able to do that any more.

G. Evans
London, SE18

SIR – As a regular traveller on British Rail, a smoking ban in restaurant and buffet areas is welcome news.

Smoking in eating areas is a despicable habit. On a number of occasions my pleasure in eating a meal has been spoilt by the smell of tobacco smoke.

There are areas provided for smokers on trains and it is

quite right that places where food is being eaten should not be among them.

Paul Adam
Bolton, Lancs.

SIR – 'No smoking' in trains. An excellent idea, happily now being extended.

How about 'no talking'? When I wish to read on the train I often find it difficult if not impossible because of talking by other passengers.

When I am with a companion and talk I feel guilty and inhibited if other passengers in the vicinity are trying to read. Some 'no smoking or talking' coaches or compartments would be a boon.

Alec Samuels
Bassett, Hants.

27 MARCH 1982

SIR – In answer to the letter by Mr Peter C. Hart (March 25) I can assure him from practical experience that there has not been any decline in business in catering vehicles on the Western Region of British Rail due to the introduction of the 'no smoking' campaign.

Fortunately the West of England route is blessed with the High Speed Train rolling stock without seating space in the buffet cars, so the passengers are inclined to make their purchases at the buffet and then return to their seats in the train and enjoy a cigarette if they wish, always assuming that they have chosen a smoking area.

As far as restaurant cars are concerned, very few people

actually smoke during a meal, but should anyone care to have coffee in a smoking area, every effort is made by myself and competent staff to accommodate him.

Being an ex-smoker I fully understand Mr Hart and would say to him: try to understand the non-smoker who, I feel, is in the majority.

Surveys have been carried out on the Western Region and I believe that there was an overwhelming number in favour of the non-smoking areas.

Should Mr Hart have the good fortune to travel on the *Golden Hind* 07.00 Plymouth to Paddington or the *Cornish Riviera* Paddington to Penzance he can do so with the safe knowledge that in no way will his meal in the restaurant car or his drink at the bar be spoiled because he cannot have a smoke.

Paul Callard
Chief Stewart, Travellers' Fare
Plymouth

SIR — Alec Samuels, besides disliking smokers, does not like 'talkers' in his train carriage (March 25).

I cannot stand people who read newspapers, books, maga-zines, letters; do office work; study; write; knit; drink; eat; chew sweets; sleep; snore; blow their noses; scratch; yawn; cough; laugh; cry or, come to that, do anything other than sit upright, with eyes open, and leave the carriage quietly making sure to close the door gently upon reaching their destination.

May I suggest that British Rail alter a large number of their carriages to single-seat accommodation in order that self-centred passengers may travel in perfect comfort.

Janet V. Price
Roxwell, Essex

12 APRIL 1982

SIR — The zealots of British Rail in their attempts to impose Social Democratic views on drinking and smoking have trapped themselves in a Byzantine muddle.

At my local station the general waiting room has been designated — 'at the request of the majority of passengers' — whoever they were — as a no-smoking area. However, it is possible to smoke in the ticket queue or while passing from the station entrance to the platform. But both of these are, in fact, in the waiting room.

But for half of the population who smoke there is an alternative to standing in the rain and cold for a relaxing smoke. The ladies' waiting room is still a smoking area. So for all the commuting chaps the answer is twofold: a complaint to the Equal Opportunities Commission and a frock in the briefcase.

Alternatively, we could return to a little sanity.

G.G. Rix
Cookham Dean, Berks.

ORDEAL BY TRANSISTOR

SIR — Railway correspondents on smoking in railway buffet cars reminds one of another form of pollution on the trains — the increasing use of cassette players and radios in open-plan carriages.

As we cannot all afford to escape it by travelling first-class, would BR try to make second-class travel less of an ordeal by installing headphone points to allow *private* listening for those who must have the 'music'.

D. Bates
Basingstoke, Hants.

11 JUNE 1983
'NO EATING' AREAS

SIR — It has been suggested that, as well as 'no smoking' areas on trains, there should be a 'no talking' compartment but I would like to propose a 'no eating' area.

If this is not possible could British Rail at least confine the eating of chips, Cornish pasty, soup and so on to the buffet?

B. Robinson
Chesterfield, Derbyshire

16 JUNE 1983
NO MEWLING, PLEASE

SIR — Neither smoking nor eating bothers me much on trains, but babies do. I am sure I am not alone.

W.H. Jarvis
Preston, Lancs.

2 JULY 1983
PAYING FOR THE TRACK

SIR — Why is the suggestion that some rail services should be run by private concerns treated as a revolutionary one?

Harbour authorities do not own shipping. Airlines do not own airports. I have yet to hear of a road haulage firm that owns a road. Is there any sound reason why rail haulage companies should own the track they use, apart from the slightly irrelevant one that they do so at the moment?

The general public has for a good few years now become used to paying the building and maintenance of roads out of taxation and the highway authorities are not asked to show a profit from their activities. Policing of highways is paid from the public purse and so are all traffic lights and controls.

Is it not a feasible proposition to operate what is left of a once good railway network on a similar basis? If the operating companies are only expected to pay for use of services supplied as do road haulage ones, and there was an element of competition over the supply of rail haulage services, it is quite conceivable that we might have fair competition between rail, road and air services.

Ross Unwin
Snettisham, Norfolk

27 AUGUST 1983
TRAVELLER'S TALE

SIR – Your comments (Aug. 24) on the Bed-Pan line encouraged me to give my trial run from Bedford. When the train did not start, various wandering around railwaymen only shrugged their lack of interest. After a time an unintelligible noise from the loudhailer caused a few hesitant passengers to get out. Then, as others followed, so, sheep-like, did I, up the long steps, over a bridge and down, a bit of a wait, and into another train. The hailer went again, which, from an adjustment, revealed a human voice, but one not used to English, and we were off.

In the smoking part, fag ends and matches were all over the floor. There were no ashtrays. And head-rests fell off without the aid of vandals. Some unkempt NUR badge-wearers in bits of uniform stood closely conversing at the carriage-end and, as we neared St Pancras, the long-haired ticket collector joined them. I thought of the splendid railwaymen of yore — and there are still some further north — neat, upright and customer conscious.

Rather than blame the long union hold-up, a little more imagination from British Rail, and seeing how they do it on the Continent, would have obviated much of the extra testing time needed. And, a lot more staff training, which I am sure the NUR would not disagree with, as it, too, cannot be unaware of the need to get travellers back from the roads.

The ride and acceleration from stops were good, but there was much noise, and at times a deafening rumble. I later asked the driver if that was when he put on the brakes. 'No,' he said, 'it's the air conditioning. It's quite a good train as long as you're not a passenger, bit light on its feet, perhaps, but can do ninety.'

E.E. Kimbell
Boughton, Northants.

3 DECEMBER 1983
LIVING MEMORIAL

SIR — May I raise a plea for the retention of the Settle to Carlisle railway line as an historical monument to an age of achievement the like of which we shall not see again. With those soaring viaducts, mighty tunnels and massive earth - works, it is surely the epitome of nineteenth century railway building in this country.

We have a National Railway Museum for the preservation of locomotives, many maintained in working order. Why not retain this line as a living memorial to the men who built it and operated it? The peaceful quiet of the water meadows of the Eden Valley, through the wooded low fells onward and upward to the awesome bleak loneliness of the moors and mountains must not be lost.

John Barnes
Windsor, Berks.

18 APRIL 1984
VITAL LINK

SIR – Mr Christopher Howse in his quite excellent article on the railway refreshment scene (April 9) omits reference to the best refreshment facility that London railway stations have to offer.

The superb Edwardian bar at Marylebone Station is an absolute gem, its comfortable ambience and good service making it a pleasanter place for a brief socialisation than most licensed premises in London, whether on railway property or otherwise.

Marylebone Station should, of course, be preserved as a vital rail link between the capital and the North-West Home Counties but the disaster that would befall us with the closure, should it ever be allowed to happen, of the station's superb refreshment facilities would outweigh even the inconvenience of having to find an alternative means of public transport.

David J. Harvey
London, SW1

21 MAY 1984
APPLAUSE, APPLAUSE

SIR – I remember quite clearly that it was quite usual for someone to walk the length of the Manchester to Euston train and thank the driver for a safe journey in 1940.

E.A. Stringer
Rochdale, Lancs.

26 MAY 1984

SIR – Mr E.A. Stringer remembers (May 21) that it was quite usual for someone to walk the length of a Manchester to Euston train to thank the driver for a safe journey in 1940.

On arrival at Euston it was, and still is, usually necessary to walk past the locomotive in order to leave the platform. And how often, I wonder, did passengers have a word with the driver or fireman, little knowing that they had only just arrived on the footplate to take the locomotive to the depot.

As often as not the mainline crew would nip away as smartly as possible to sign off duty.

P.L. Lynch
Pinner, Middlesex

18 SEPTEMBER 1984
INTER-CITY SQUALOR

SIR – What is happening at British Rail Inter-City? I took a trip to Norwich on Sept. 10, returning to London the following day, and on both journeys experienced every sign of incompetence and squalor.

The train was 20 minutes late leaving Liverpool Street because, as the announcer said: 'We are looking for the engine.'

Most of the ashtrays in the first-class smoking compar - tment were either broken or filled with cigarette butts. The carpet was filthy and the toilets were blocked. The only toilet that was clean and working was marked: 'Not open to the public. For staff only.' No hot food was available during the return journey.

On its way back to London, the train stopped for half an hour because another train was blocking the track. During another, unaccountably, long stop I asked a guard if I could get out and pick some flowers.

'I don't see any flowers,' he said.

'But I have a packet of seeds,' I replied.

Jacqueline Harman
London, W8

24 SEPTEMBER 1984

SIR – Miss Jacqueline Harman ('What is happening to British Rail Inter-City?'), on the basis of her return journey to Norwich, complains of 'incompetence and squalor'.

My wife and I have this year made a number of Inter-City journeys, both first and second class, and our experience has been wholly different from that of Miss Harman. The trains were clean and comfortable, the staff most helpful, the catering reasonable, and all journeys both fast and smooth, some even ahead of schedule.

On the same day as Miss Harman travelled to Norwich we returned from Liverpool to Brighton, including the Underground interchange between Euston and Victoria, in less than four hours! It would have taken at least twice as long by road and been far more wearing.

J.H. Francis
Brighton

SIR – Miss Jacqueline Harman's lengthy delays on Norwich to London trains are nothing new. That route was originally the preserve of the Great Eastern Railway, about which many apocryphal stories have been told, usually on the subject of timekeeping.

One concerned a diligent ticket collector who accused a youth of 16 of travelling half-price, only to be told by the latter that he had been 12 when the train started!

Nothing changes . . .

H.I. Quayle
Felixstowe, Suffolk

25 SEPTEMBER 1984

SIR – I was most concerned to read (Sept. 18) of the difficulties experienced by Miss Jacqueline Harman on her journey to and from Norwich.

The delay to the Norwich train on Sept. 10 was as a result of emergency repair work on a broken rail near Hatfield Peverel. This delayed the arrival of incoming rolling stock and locomotives at Liverpool Street and routine cleaning of carriages suffered because of the shortened turn-round time.

While I can appreciate the irritation of passengers who find one of the toilets labelled for staff use only, it is a statutory requirement to provide this facility for catering staff.

On Miss Harman's return journey hot food was not available because of a faulty gas cylinder. Regrettably this train was then delayed when a preceding freight train broke down near Ipswich.

I must apologise for the inconvenience suffered by Miss Harman but the poor impression she gained from a combination of unfortunate circumstances do not reflect the normal high standard of our main-line services.

J.B. Ellis
Asst Gen. Manager (South), British Rail
London, EC2

20 NOVEMBER 1984
FORWARD THE RAILWAYS!

SIR – I was delighted to read (report, Nov. 12) of a proposal to expand the usage of the railway network by permitting private operators to run trains over British Rail track.

Why should one of our greatest national assets remain under-used? Why should the safest method of land-based transport be penalised by the financial burden of maintaining its own track and policing its own safety?

The road operators don't have this worry. (Imagine the difficulty that the National Bus Company would have, trying to maintain its own private road network.)

This country has already lost too many railway lines and stations through false interpretation of accounts. 'Loss-making' lines have been identified and axed, but the fact that the closure of these lines failed to stem British Rail's losses gave the lie to this argument. Their closure simply took customers away from the rest of the rail network.

You cannot improve the sales of a business by removing

sales outlets and services offered. You have to offer more of them and make them better.

Competition between road and rail transport would be more meaningful if both were placed on an equal financial footing and I welcome this proposal as a means of offering a safer and more competitive transport system to the public.

T.L. Davies
Tettenhall, West Midlands

29 NOVEMBER 1985
TRAINED TO MAKE MAXIMUM IMPACT

SIR – British Rail's orders for new rolling stock, electri-fication and improvements to catering and facilities at stations etc., costing millions of pounds of public money, are never going to be helped by the fact that much needed revenue is being lost because the collection of fares/issue of tickets appears to be a thing of the past, certainly on the suburban services of North London.

It is utterly pointless to have countless staff delaying commuter passengers in particular, ostensibly to examine and collect tickets at, for instance, Finsbury Park and London termini, when travel between stations is totally out of control. The absence of station staff at intermediate stations encourages short bookings to cover quite lengthy journeys, and many passengers not to book at all.

Twice recently I could have climbed aboard trains and left at intermediate stations without having paid a penny piece or seeing any station staff. On one memorable occasion when I went looking for staff in the platform staff room and enquired if someone could sell me a ticket, I must have made myself very noticeable for the train emptied with passengers lining up behind me to purchase tickets.

I do suggest, therefore, that staff could be better employed examining tickets and collecting fares *on the trains* where considerable losses are being incurred, if the proper man - ning of stations is too costly or presents too many problems.

Anthony Bath
Cromer, Herts.

30 MARCH 1986 (ST)
HIGH-SPEED CHUNNEL QUESTIONS

SIR – Ian Waller's article on the Channel Tunnel was a tour de force on the potential role for rail. The greater the contribution of 'classic' rail, and the further that direct European rail passenger and freight services extend through Britain, the better for the environment, the British economy and the project.

There are, however, obstacles in the path of a greater railway involvement in this country.

Assuming – and it is a big if – that environmental issues can be reconciled, it is vital that the rest of Britain should have through passenger trains. BR estimates that nearly 65 per cent of all potential Chunnel rail passengers will start or finish their journeys outside London and the South-East, with nearly 40 per cent from the Midlands and the North. But a good range of through trains will only be possible if HM Customs & Excise agree to on-train examination.

Through rail freight links with continental Europe and beyond – container trains can go as far as China – will create the opportunity for 'conveyor belt' goods links across the Channel with new direct outlets for British products. This needs adequate investment in private sidings and new wagons, yet the Government's grant-aid scheme for rail freight facilities (called the Section 8 grant) has a strict cash limit.

Transport Minister David Mitchell told the London Regional Passengers Committee on March 26 that he 'warmly welcomed' the opportunity the Channel Tunnel presented 'for taking juggernauts off our roads'. If he really believes this, the Department of Transport should remove the shackles of cash limits on the Section 8 procedures and ensure that the rail can remove the juggernaut from our roads.

Jonathan Roberts
Deputy Director, Transport 2000
London, NW1

SIR – As a life-long railway enthusiast I was very interested in Ian Waller's article on the Channel Tunnel. I have doubts about a dual voltage system of electric traction for such a large project, and I think BR would be wise to extend the 25KV AC system with overhead conductors from Willesden Junction, where it already exists, to Cheriton.

It was indeed unfortunate that Sir Herbert Walker and his electrical engineers on the former Southern Railway should have decided in 1926 to scrap a similar AC system with overhead conductors originated in 1909 by the London Brighton & South Coast Railway, and which by 1926 had reached a third of the way to Brighton.

Robert Perkins
London, E1

SIR – A major question worries me about the Channel Tunnel project. Why, if the cars and lorries will be carried on rail through the tunnel, is it not arranged for the pickaback to be extended each side from the M25 on the English side close to BR's main line, and Lille on the French, so as to spare Kent the road traffic with its smells and vibration?

It would avoid the cost of extensions on the M2 and M20 to Folkestone.

R.G.R. Calvert
Truro, Cornwall

1 AUGUST 1986
LEVEL CROSSING SOLUTION?

SIR – Surely the problem with level crossings is not the way they are left unguarded but that they are level. If they were not level any vehicle could run under gravity off them.

It seems to me, therefore, that the roadway over the crossing for a distance of about 20 metres either side should be divided down the middle with a barrier so that traffic is physically separated. Then ramps down to and away from the rails could be built at a slight slope, say 1:20, beginning within centimetres of the steel rails in the direction of the motor traffic. Any vehicle coming to rest actually on the rails is the only one at risk until it is pushed say with its starter motor and in first gear a few metres until the ramp and gravity take over.

It would also help if the ramps were very smooth to reduce as far as possible the road surface friction. Putting sleepers across the rail road area is not conducive to safety because they provide a rough ride just when a smooth one is desperately needed.

Once the essential road gradients are established the levels can be reconnected to the original road over acceptable distances such as 50 metres.

Alan Lovegreen
Wallingford, Oxon.

24 NOVEMBER 1986
GETTING THERE

SIR – I recently spent a two month vacation in Britain and travelled by British Rail between London, Aberdeen, Ayr and back to London.

It is 15 years since I used to commute between Hertfordshire and London and was used to the dingy stations and trains. Imagine my delight on finding that my local station had received a complete face lift and its appearance was bright.

At King's Cross I had to pick up my sleeper reservation not from some dingy booking hall but from a bright modern office called a 'travel centre'. My wife and I travelled economy class and had a comfortable compartment to ourselves. The rolling stock was newish, well sound-insulated and with welded rails we glided through the night smoothly sleeping.

On arriving at Aberdeen we stepped out on to a newly laid, bright clean concourse where we had breakfast at a 'Travel Fare' Cafe not a flyblown buffet.

Our next trip was Aberdeen to Ayr via Glasgow, again in newish carriages, with a rolling buffet service. Everything was on time.

Our journey back to London by an Inter City train was excellent, arriving at Euston 15 min. early. There were two stops on the way but in spite of this the train averaged 110 m.p.h.!

Believe me, compared with Amtrak on the east coast of the US, Britain should be proud of its railway efforts.

L. Melhuish
Aberdeen, North Carolina

22 MARCH 1987 (ST)
DIRTY TRAINS

SIR – What a pity Ian Watson had to mar an otherwise excellent article 'How Will Lawson Divide the Spoils of Recovery?' with a little 'dig' about dirty trains. I really do wonder where he travels by train or, indeed, how extensively he does so. Perhaps he commutes in the inner-London area south of the Thames; if so, I would grant him that some dirty and uncouth citizens on the same route leave dirt and litter on *some* trains.

Journalists, however, discredit themselves by having blinkered vision, and I challenge Ian Watson to travel by train widely over other areas of the country, as I do, because in my experience it is a great rarity to find trains that are other than clean, warm or comfortable.

I hope he will then feel constrained to write in a more balanced way on this subject.

P. Reed
Reading

26 MAY 1987

NATIONAL CONTRACTS

SIR – Attitudes of mind. Here we are with British Railways proposing the closure of the 72-mile Settle and Carlisle railway because they can't afford to maintain the structure and, at the same time, French Railways are proposing to build a new 75-mile high-speed electrified line through similar, but perhaps more difficult country, to the east of Lyon. Words fail me!

A.F. Buckland
Brigsteer, Cumbria

1 AUGUST 1987

NAME AND DECAY

SIR – If ever evidence were needed of Britain's decline into mediocrity, British Rail can provide it. This morning I saw an Inter-City locomotive carrying the nameplate: *Municipal County of Tyne and Wear*!

'Oh my *Mallard* and my *Flying Scotsman* . . .'

F.C. Smart
Cheadle Hulme, Cheshire

6 APRIL 1988

ONLY DWARFS ESCAPE SPRINTER SUFFERING

SIR – It is my great misfortune – and no doubt the great misfortune of other travellers – that British Rail have introduced a totally misnamed train called the Sprinter. It is without doubt the most uncomfortable train ever put into service.

The seats are designed for the use of thin dwarfs – short-legged ones at that! It is impossible to walk down a carriage whilst the train is moving without being thrown into the laps of surprised fellow passengers.

The provision for passengers' luggage is totally inadequate, and the genius responsible for the design of this train, in his infinite wisdom, failed to provide any litter bins or ashtrays. The result being that this horror of a train becomes a travelling trash can.

British Rail, you have made a mistake. Please go back to the drawing board.

Lady Ropner
Bedale, North Yorks.

1 APRIL 1989
ROLLING DOWN TO WALES

SIR – As I read in Commentary (Mar. 27) that 'the efficiency of all transport systems, public or private, depends ultimately on customers not taking things lying down', I recalled the remark to me of a member of Lord Robertson's Railway Board just after the 1939–1945 War to the effect that 'we always send our second-best rolling stock to Wales because the Welsh don't complain'.

A.M. Man
Narberth, Dyfed

6 JULY 1989
ANTIPODEAN ANSWER

SIR – I understand that in Australia striking rail workers continue to operate trains but fail to collect the fares. I wonder is it too much to ask both BR and the NUR to agree to similar *modus operandi* and thereby spare the travelling public the agony of their political indulgence?

David Uren
Romsey, Hants.

7 JULY 1989
WHY SO DOCILE?

SIR – A Canadian who has lived in this country for 22 years, I never cease to be amazed by the quiescence of its travelling millions in the face of miseries such as those now being heaped upon them.

Strikes, cancellations, cattle-car congestion and other perpetrations are borne with a sort of seemly silence. The slightest outburst of exasperation heard across a platform, rail carriage or bus is treated by the majority as something not done. Conditions that would spark passenger riots elsewhere are endured without complaint, day in, day out, by this stoic throng.

Is this prodigious passivity a legacy of the wartime spirit of 'We Can Take It'? Does it reflect some masochistic racial quirk? Or is it, instead, the result of a collective emasculation effected as a part of the taming of a great nation?

C.J. Fox
Sydenham

12 MARCH 1991

TAKE A BRANCH LINE TO SECOND PLACE

SIR – This letter may come as a surprise to Mr Ron Westerby, Chief Education Officer of Labour-controlled Dudley, who is banning *Postman Pat* and *Thomas the Tank Engine* books from 85 nursery and primary schools because of their macho male stereotypes (report, March 2).

I am one female who doesn't care one jot that all the engines in the Rev. W. Awdry's books are male (dirty, smelly old engines, anyway).

If Mr Westerby is so concerned about 'men leading and women following' perhaps he could leave poor Thomas the Tank Engine alone and think about his own job. He could always accept a lesser position and let some female become chief education officer. I am sure there must be many who would be delighted to have the opportunity.

Who knows, unlike Mr Westerby, she may be gifted with common sense and put *Postman Pat* and *Thomas the Tank Engine* books back in the nursery and primary school shelves where they so rightly belong.

Brenda Narraway
Bedford

18 OCTOBER 1991

SHORT NEGLECT

SIR – I live only eight miles outside London on the Bexleyheath/Barnehurst line and it is one of the worst in the capital.

The trains are invariably dirty, late and always crowded. Indeed, when on one occasion a clean train pulled into Charing

Cross for the return journey, the passengers hesitated to get on, being unable to believe that it could be bound for Bexleyheath and Barnehurst. They had to check with the guards.

There have been no such clean trains since.

Colline Mcleod
London, SE3

6 NOVEMBER 1991
LEAVES ON THE LINE

SIR- As a graduate of the Royal College of Public Excuses I deplore the decline in the standard of BR's excuses (report, Nov. 4). 'Autumn leaves' — I ask you. Our railway system has existed for more than 150 years — time enough, one would think, for British Rail and its predecessors to have noticed the tendency of leaves to fade and fall in autumn, and to devise remedial action.

I therefore suggest miniature wheels on specially designed all-weather rail-cleaning trains to brush the leaves away. First clean could be at, say, 4 a.m. and thereafter hourly.

There could also be a continuous supply of nocturnal leaf-eating creatures and leaf-collecting birds which would, of course, be clearly marked 'property of British Rail'.

As for excuses for other seasons, for spring I recommend 'rails overgrown by bindweed, ground elder, etc.'; 'massive invasion of moles and voles undermining the tracks'; 'rare orchids and other wild flowers discovered on railway tracks'; or 'snails on tracks'. For summer there could be 'heatwave buckling the metal tracks'.

Eric Davis
London, NW11

WHERE BRUNEL WENT OFF THE RAILS

SIR – Was any reputation for outstanding technical innovation less well deserved than that of Isambard Brunel (article, May 23)? His alleged achievements and engineering derring-do have been near mythologised by relentless repetition of his own accounts of events, despite the clearest contrary evidence, as in Ross Clark's panegyric rehearsal of the way the Master's superior vision of broad gauge was rejected by an ungrateful nation in favour of a Geordie blacksmith's coal waggon standard.

Brunel's unfortunate effect is best illustrated by the anonymity of his often far more talented successors. How many can name the man responsible for the engineering of the Severn Tunnel project, or the Manchester Ship Canal, or any other major innovatory work of the post-Brunel era? Since Brunel, the working engineer has been kept very much in his place and out of public sight, to the national detriment as much as his own.

The broad-gauge story is the most monstrously irrational of the Brunel myths. While Stephenson foresaw and prepared for the eventual connection of the widely separated first railways, Brunel had no grand vision of a high-speed, one-gauge, worldwide system, whatever L.T.C. Rolt, Ross Clark and others believe.

His thinking was perversely parochial. He set out to fit his carriages with enormous wheels, which he supposed would give a smoother ride, and, because it would be impracticable to raise the carriages high enough to accommodate his oversize wheels underneath, he proposed to move the wheels further apart until the carriages (and passengers) could be lowered between them. Thus, the oft eulogised broad gauge 'vision' was conceived.

Remembering that early carriages based on the stagecoach were only two or three compartments long, it is not surprising that the sheer stupidity of Brunel's thinking was immediately apparent, but it is typical of Brunel that he persisted with his own peculiar gauge even after his reasons for it had been discredited, and despite the seemingly overriding advantages of national conformity.

However, Brunel was always fortunate in his associates and, guided by Daniel Gooch (who, incidentally, learned his trade from Stephenson) he later adopted more convincing sounding reasons to justify saddling his railway with a feature which not only confined it to the West Country but incurred many additional expenses, including a far more substantial arrangement of timbers to support the low-quality iron rails in use at the time.

This, with Gooch's brilliant engines, was the real secret of the broad gauge's brief initial speed advantage, and even this soon disappeared with the introduction of the steel rail.

A. Southeran
Bristol

5 JUNE 1992
AIR OF VICTORY ON THE 7.27

SIR – As a long-suffering British Rail customer, I could only sympathise with an irate lady on the 7.27 stopping service from Brighton to Victoria.

We had ground to a halt at Three Bridges due to 'traction failure', and a muffled voice advised us to cross the platform and join the London Bridge train. One woman passenger thundered up the platform in search of someone appropriate to savage and caught sight of an unusually smart gentleman in uniform who was casually leaning out of my carriage window.

'Every day of the week you people make my life a misery,' she barked. 'I don't want to change bleeping trains for the umpteenth time – when are you going to get this one moving?' Unmoved, and with commendable politeness, the gentleman replied: 'I wouldn't know that, madam. I'm an airline pilot.'

Mike Casey
Brighton, E. Sussex

12 JULY 1992 (ST)
BR ON WRONG LINES

SIR – In 1992 on British Rail I got on a train at King's Cross and got out at Aberdeen. No change necessary. In 1997 under Britain's railway utopia by private enterprise (report, July 5), I have to change trains at Edinburgh. A refusal by private enterprise to co-operate for the benefit of the passenger?

F. Manley
London, SW15

SIR – It is a misrepresentation of the policy of my union to suggest (July 5) that Aslef is 'ready to endorse the plans' to introduce private operators on British Rail.

Indeed, Aslef is committed to use every means at its disposal to oppose the privatisation of the railway industry. We fear that the Government's plans will fragment the national network, compromise safety standards, result in the closure of rural lines and stations, and accelerate job losses.

We may eventually find ourselves in a position where

franchises are forced upon us; but will never support the destruction of the publicly owned railway service.

Lew Adams
Assistant General Secretary, ASLEF
London, NW3

15 JULY 1992
BORING NAME

SIR — As a lifelong railway enthusiast I was not only disappointed by the banality of the name Le Shuttle (article, July 9), but disgusted by the amount of money that Eurotunnel spent on it — especially as the French government, under pressure from the Académie Française (which has considerable political clout), may possibly disallow it as a piece of blatant Franglais.

It is strange that no one thought of using the traditional Golden Arrow/Flèche d'Or for the London–Paris service, as this is a historical name free of any patents.

Harry Pitts
Cowplain, Hants

SIR — The name Le Shuttle fails to take into account the well-known difficulty of the French with the British short 'u'. One envisages hordes of Clouseaux arriving here aboard 'Le Shirtle'.

Stewart Hine
Harrow, Middlesex

8 DECEMBER 1992
FARE COP?

SIR – I am finding it almost impossible to pay British Rail my fare. Travelling recently from Guildford to Waterloo in the afternoon, I found there was no ticket office open, no porter to provide me with a written ticket, and the imposing-looking ticket machine would not provide me with a senior citizen ticket.

I obtained a permit to travel from another machine and eagerly expected an inspector to board the train and provide me with a proper ticket. No one appeared. At Waterloo the excess fare offices on the platforms were closed and there was no ticket collector on the gate, or indeed on any of the adjacent gates. There were no BR staff on the vast concourse at Waterloo.

Having frightened me to death with advertisements that tell me what will happen if I do not pay my fare, why is British Rail conspiring to prevent me from paying it?

Rowland Fereday
London, SW1

10 DECEMBER 1992

SIR – There is an easy solution to Mr Fereday's problem of paying his rail fare, as I discovered after a run-in with the 'Customers' Services' office (letter, Dec. 8).

Unless and until the ticket machines allow the purchase of pensioners' tickets, we can use the 'Child Return' tickets, which cost exactly the same.

Anthony Marsh
London, SE3

7 APRIL 1993
BR TAKES A PROFIT BY NEW RULES

SIR – After being subjected to millions of pounds' worth of British Rail public relations exercises, I have just re-confirmed what most commuters know anyway: inefficiency and petty officialdom are still thriving in the organisation.

On a recent journey from Westcombe Park (where it was impossible to buy a ticket) to Charing Cross, I discovered a Catch-22 situation designed to profit Network SouthEast. When I alighted at Charing Cross and asked for a single ticket, a menacing ticket inspector informed me that a penalty clause system was in operation.

His rudeness increased when I reminded him that I was a 'customer' and had already been inconvenienced and delayed by not being able to buy a ticket.

The unfriendly little man in an officious little suit eventually relented and sold me a ticket at the correct price. But only after I told him I would call a policeman and complain that he was trying to perpetrate a fraud or demanding money with menaces.

Patrick Prentice
London, SE10

18 APRIL 1993 (ST)
THIS FARCE IS NOT THE TICKET AT ALL

SIR – My wife and I want to travel from Geneva to Venice by train this month.

Being a reasonably prudent traveller I concluded I should book in London in order to ensure seats.

Visits to numerous travel agents – Swiss Rail, British Rail,

French Railways, Thomas Cook, etc. – elicited exactly the same response: 'So sorry, we can't help you – since we entered the single market, quotas have been established and we are precluded from making bookings in Europe unless you originate in London.' What is the point of Europe? I shall have to telephone friends in Geneva and ask them to book for me. What a farce.

Gordon Wilson
London, SW1

14 MAY 1993
FIRST AMONG THE TRAINSPOTTERS

SIR – While I can understand Anthony Gardner's efforts to prove that it is possible to be highly gifted academically and still be a 'normal' individual (letter, May 11), as a lifelong enthusiast I protest at the notion of trainspotters being at the lower end of the intelligence scale.

Among my own circle are a chartered accountant and a research chemist. Both are certainly keen rail fans. Just as in music – all three of us enjoy 'serious music' – the field in the study of railways is enormous: social history, architecture, photography, industrial development, geography – to name but a few.

Of course there are many dumb number-takers, but I feel it is about time somebody spoke up for the enormous number of people who make the study of railways a serious hobby and still lead a 'normal' life.

George Whetton
Belper, Derbys.

26 MAY 1993
SUPER(FACE)SAVER

SIR – I can think of a motive for the Government heading off a rail revolt (report, May 25). Read in a British Rail announcer's voice it goes: 'We regret that rail privatisation plans will be delayed because politicians' popularity is on the line.'

Graham Stubbs
Berkhamsted, Herts.

DULL VIEW FOR TGV PASSENGERS

SIR – There is no need for Lord Deedes (Commentary, May 24) to feel embarrassed by French jibes about the cautious progress of our Channel tunnel rail link.

The TGV link from Paris to the French entrance to the tunnel passes through a thinly populated and scenically uninspiring (to put it mildly) region of north-eastern France.

Any British high-speed line must pass through the densely populated 'Garden of England'. Moreover, the French, in their collective quest for *la gloire*, are more prepared to ride roughshod over individual property rights than is customary in this country.

Finally, the purchase of a TGV ticket at a Paris terminus can take almost as long as the journey itself. To make life a misery for people obliged to live near a high-speed line is even less justified if the total point-to-point time – including the time spent at stations – represents only a marginal improvement.

Lord Monson
London, SW1

THE BILL THAT CANNOT WORK

SIR – The Railways (Privatisation) Bill is due its second reading in the House of Lords next week. Many of us, whose companies are members of the Railway Industries' Association, favour privatisation and would normally support it.

However, I sense that it may not be fully understood outside the industry, how this privatisation Bill is different from its forebears. It is not about transporting and marketing energy products, telecommunications or water – competitively. It is about moving people and freight on one of the world's highest density rail systems – competitively.

Most Bills, which pass through the Second Chamber to become law, do not have to rely on sophisticated technology or specialist operators to become workable. The Railways Bill does, and, in the form sent up by the House of Commons, must be deemed unworkable by the private sector on operational grounds alone.

It is also unworkable because it does not incorporate a proper business plan or guarantee to franchisees the necessary and ongoing public funding of rolling stock replacement and track improvements. Forty thousand jobs in the railway industry must be at risk because of these omissions.

On the other hand, if the entire rail network is to be privatised, 140,000 legal contracts may have to be negotiated with the franchisees once this Bill becomes law.

Similarly, the Department of Transport may have to expand its activities dramatically, in order to adjudicate, explain and negotiate the 140,000 franchise agreements to potential franchisees.

I wonder if there is any way whereby this unfortunate Railways Bill can be quietly put into cold storage – with honour and without loss of face by the Government? Is there any other way that British Rail can be privatised without further delay to the capital renewal programme and the job losses this will entail?

Surely privatisation is intended to be, as John Major described it to the CBI last month, a partnership between state and industry – not a sop for the Civil Service and the legal profession as set out in the current Railways Bill?

Lord Tanlaw
London, SW1

18 AUGUST 1993

PROBLEMS RIGHT DOWN THE LINE

SIR – As W.F. Deedes's realistic assessment (article, Aug. 17) clearly points out, the ill-considered nature of the Government's rail privatisation plans bear all the seeds of a disaster: fragmentation of the network will present considerable logistical and safety problems.

Consider, for example, one London terminus, Liverpool Street. This will serve at least four franchises covering a large number of destinations, including those of a busy commuter network: at least three of the franchises, including the commuter network, will share common tracks at least to Colchester. Who will decide on the running priorities of each franchise? Further, a breakdown in one franchise could affect all others.

What alternative arrangements will be made? Would passengers have redress against one franchise-holder, even if they were travelling with another? At present passengers to some destinations out of Liverpool Street have a choice of services; doubtless this will no longer be so under privatisation.

How many tickets will a passenger have to buy if his journey involves several franchises? This plan poses a traveller's nightmare.

And while the Transport Minister has stated that privatisation will improve services to passengers, his department seems reticent in providing factual evidence from other rail networks that this is so.

Unfortunately, this 'caring' government is not and never has been a 'listening' government, and will take not the slightest notice of W.F. Deedes's views or the doubts expressed by other authoritative individuals and organisations.

A.W. Huish
Ilford, Essex

20 AUGUST 1993

SIR – Congratulations to W.F. Deedes (article, Aug. 17) on his concise destruction of the case for rail privatisation, and for identifying its co-sponsors: the privatise-everything clique, making common cause with a Treasury which wants to get British Rail 'off the Government's ledger'.

In the short term, a few model franchisees would have money thrown at them, to demonstrate that fragmented privatisation can work. But unless there is to be a substantial net increase in Treasury funding – which is clearly not the Government's intention – this must be at the expense of the remainder of the network, still operated for the foreseeable future by BR.

The proposed abolition of Inter-City, to be divided among 14 different franchisees, illustrates the fiscal reck-lessness of what is being done. At present Inter-City, on the basis of internal cross-subsidy, has the distinction of being the only profitable rail network in Europe. But franchise off the profitable parts and overnight a whole new group of subsidy-dependent lines will have been created. In whose interest is that?

W.F. Deedes is right to point out that private franchisees will 'have the Government over a barrel' in demanding higher subsidy if fare increases and service cuts are to be avoided. Rail privatisation is a party political issue and will remain so.

But it is also one on which party allegiances have already been transcended on the basis of rational argument. From April, BR will be operating trains they do not own on tracks they do not own. Is that the way to run a railway — or to ensure accountability by those who do?

Brian Wilson, MP (Lab)
London, SW1

23 SEPTEMBER 1993
END OF THE LINE?

SIR — I spotted the new British Rail winter timetable, just published, in the 'Puzzles and Comics' section of John Menzies bookshop at Manchester Piccadilly Railway Station.

David Kane
Hope, Derbyshire

6 NOVEMBER 1993

UP THE JUNCTION

SIR — The Government's scramble to pass the unwanted Railways Bill was rich in irony (report, Nov. 4). As the Bill was shunted between the two houses at Westminster, you could almost hear the announcement: 'We apologise for the late arrival of this legislation, which has been caused by the wrong kind of peers.'

For reasons of efficiency, the Government must have been wishing it had total control of the legislative process at that point. It's an interesting thought, given that the Bill's objective is to split up the railways between numerous operators, thus rendering planning and overall control of the system more of a nightmare than it is at present.

I fear the chaos in Parliament is only a taste of the confusion to come on the trains, as a result of what Robert Adley, the late and much lamented Conservative MP, dubbed 'a poll tax on wheels'.

Ivor Wason
Liverpool

21 MARCH 1994

HAUNTING MYSTERY OF TRAIN TRAGEDY

SIR — Elizabeth Grice's article (March 8) about the ease with which people can disappear reminds me of the utterly baffling case of two young children killed in a railway accident in Charfield, Gloucestershire, in October 1928, when the Leeds—Bristol express crashed into a goods train and burst into flames. All 16 casualties were identified except for a boy aged 12 and a girl of about 6, both badly burned.

The ticket collector, who survived the crash, remembered seeing two children board the train alone at Gloucester. He said they were wearing school hats. Part of a breast pocket of a school blazer was found, with a school motto, *Luce Magistra*, as well as two new 9-inch-long shoes and part of a sock with the initials CSSS.

Yet tailors and shoemakers over a large area were canvassed without result. Schools, churches, advertisements yielded not a single clue.

Surely someone was waiting for them at the first and only stop? No result there. No relative, friend, teacher, neighbour reported or knew of them. The strangeness of this has haunted me ever since. Ultimately they were buried, the railway company taking responsibility for the formalities. Unbelievable but true.

Harold Wilkinson
Sturminster Newton, Dorset

4 MAY 1994
ON THE SLOW LINE

SIR – Like many job-hungry students I spent a good deal of my Christmas vacation applying to a wide variety of employers in anticipation of my graduation this summer.

One such application was to join the rail industry of the future ('We are embarking on a journey – so are you?'). I was fortunate enough to be selected for interview – no mean feat if you have seen the application form. I went on to one of their assessment centres in early April. We were told that an offer of employment, or not as the case may be, would get to us within a couple of weeks.

I still have not heard, and telephone inquiries result only

in the advice that notification will be with applicants as soon as possible. Clearly things are running a little late at the train operating companies, and I wonder to what extent this might typify any future career. Could I turn up for employment a couple of weeks after the starting date? Will a slower pace of work be allowed during peak commuting hours?

Perhaps I should not be too concerned. I haven't yet been given a reservation for the journey. And in any case, nobody seems to know the destination.

Gary Page
Lancaster University

14 JULY 1994
RAILWAY SLEEPERS

SIR – The weekly rail strikes seem to have given the phrase 'taking a Knapp' new meaning.

Tim Fox
Beckenham, Kent

13 AUGUST 1994
PROMPT IN DISPUTE

SIR – Long may the present rail dispute continue! In all my years of commuting, I have never experienced such a consistently reliable and punctual service as that on the strike days.

In contrast on the 'normal' days on my Southern Region line from Epsom or Effingham Junction to Waterloo, I have experienced cancellations and delays. On three consecutive evenings this week alone, the service has been 13, 18 and 10 minutes late.

Roll on Monday and Tuesday! I will take holiday the rest of the week as BR is threatening to operate its normal service.

M.W. Alexander
Great Bookham, Surrey

9 JANUARY 1995
TICKETS PLEASE

SIR — Your report '50-mile trip to buy new rail tickets' (Jan. 7) reminds me of a similar situation nine years ago when I was returning from a visit to my ancestral home in the Punjab, and my cousin had to make the round trip from Jullundur to Amritsar in order to book us on a train to Delhi.

This crazy piece of bureaucracy, which for all I know still persists, seems likely to have its counterpart here in the future. But I doubt if any of the new companies will invest ticket-collectors with the importance they have in India, where the 'TC Sahib' is much too grand actually to clip your ticket (a minion accompanies him to do this), and bears a closer resemblance to the major-domo of a rather snobbish and down-at-heel club.

The principal function of a ticket-collector on British trains will no doubt continue to be that of waking up sleeping passengers. On a coach — one mode of transport where privatisation has worked — one is not only spared this indignity, but also pays less.

George Chowdharay-Best
London, SW3

26 JANUARY 1995
THROUGH-TICKETING ALREADY HALTED

SIR – Dr Brian Mawhinney's protests about the maintenance of through-ticketing (report, Jan. 19) have a hollow ring for those of us in the West Country who use rail to get to London.

Like many others I frequently go up to town through Waterloo, which is convenient for the City, then return through the West End and Paddington, stopping off at Bristol or Oxford on the return journey.

However, it is now no longer possible to buy a through ticket for this simple journey. The two companies operating the alternative routes to London have ceased accepting each others' tickets. The journey now requires at least two tickets which cost twice as much as the most commonly used return ticket on the old system.

Nor does the split between the companies end there.

On Exeter St David's station recently I looked at a timetable for a train to Paignton. To my amazement Paddington did not appear – nor did Torquay! Station staff pointed out to me that there are now no fewer than three operating timetables in different parts of the station, one for each of the new companies using it.

To Mr Major's credit it appears that he did originally back a scheme based on the existing companies InterCity, Network SouthEast and Regional Railways. This might have worked, although the plight of Railtrack is not encouraging.

The present proposals will not do. They must in some way be stopped before the damage already being inflicted is rendered irreversible. Pleas that there is a manifesto commitment, or that there is no alternative, will have to be ignored, however embarrassing another U-turn might seem to be.

W.J. West
Exeter

8 APRIL 1995
SPONSOR A SMOKING CARRIAGE

SIR – If Lord Harris of High Cross wishes to smoke on Network South-East services (report, April 7) he could do worse than adapt to the market-driven environment in which British Rail now operates.

As chairman of Forest, an organisation linked to the amply resourced tobacco industry, he should perhaps consider organising a commercial consortium to operate smokers' carriages on normal services.

A Benson and Hedges smokers' carriage, for instance, could possibly charge lower fares than a non-smoking one if seat occupancy rates are higher due to relative scarcity – if only 20 per cent of a train is smoking when 30 per cent of the population smoke. Even though cleaning costs might be higher, a franchise could install some serious ashtray technology.

H.T. Mackenzie
Sevenoaks, Kent

19 APRIL 1995
WRONG LINES

SIR – You report that the rail operator Eastern Cross Country is experiencing overcrowding on the Portsmouth–Cardiff line (April 14). As the operator apparently cannot afford further rolling stock it intends to ban Network cards and discount tickets on Fridays. You quote the manager, Mr Chris Gibb, explaining: 'Because of the worsening problem, I will have to seek additional ways of suppressing demand for these trains.'

Such an attitude defies belief. There can surely be very few, if any, companies which have achieved success by actively seeking to deter customers by making their services less attractive.

Rail operators must resolve the 'problem' by any means necessary. They must start finding ways to accommodate passengers rather than adopting the easy and defeatist route of deterring them. To do otherwise augurs ill for the future of our railways.

John L. Hinkley
Newcastle upon Tyne

20 MAY 1995

WHEELED RECOVERY

SIR — Can we not solve the problems of the Health Service and the railways in one fell swoop? Hospital trains! Three or four trains, or more, equipped as hospitals, constantly rolling around this green and pleasant land. Stops could be made where more beds are needed, to allow those who had recovered to get off to bury the dead.

What a joy 'old people's home' trains would be! A constant change of scene, and we could wave at our aged relatives as they trundled through a convenient 'home' station once a week, or less frequently. *Le Shuttle* takes on a new raft of meaning.

Canon Cedric Catton
Exning, Suffolk

3 SEPTEMBER 1995 (ST)
HI-TECH ANORAK

SIR — I read with amusement the report about train-spotting becoming the latest victim of computerisation (Aug. 27). It seems the next logical step is to put bar-codes on all the trains. Then the enthusiastic spotter would just have to stand on the platform, armed with his palm-top and suitable bar-code reader, in order to catch all the trains whizzing or wheezing past.

If the spotter were to go on the Internet then he could find out the locations of all the trains on all the networks without even having to brave the always draughty platform, as I understand the Internet is faster and more reliable than Inter-City.

Wendy L. Wood
Abbots Langley, Herts.

9 OCTOBER 1995
DO COMPLAIN

SIR — Mr Graham (letter, Sept. 25) can easily solve his problem with mobile phone yuppies on trains by directing them to make their calls from the nearest lavatory. A formal complaint that he is not paying British Rail for the privilege of travelling to work in somebody else's office can also be effective.

Mr Graham's final recourse should be to the ticket inspector — British Rail has sufficient by-laws to permit them to act if they consider that a 'public nuisance' is being committed.

Richard Longfield
Weston Patrick, Hants.

25 NOVEMBER 1995
FAMILIAR PHRASES

SIR – You may be interested to know that British Rail is again adding to its seemingly endless list of excuses for putting its 'customers' through purgatory.

Earlier this week there was a large-scale points failure at Blackfriars which of course devastated trains leaving from Victoria and Cannon Street. This problem was compounded by 'traction problems in rural areas' (leaves on the line) and 'displacement of train drivers' (the trains and their drivers were in different places). I look forward to more imaginative uses of the English language.

I also heard a conversation between a disgruntled lady 'customer' who asked a porter (if that's what they still call them) where she could find a British Rail Supervisor. The porter's reply was: 'I've no idea, but if you find one please let me know because I want a word with him.'

Martin French
Wormshill, Kent

13 MARCH 1997
SWITZERLAND ON TIME

SIR – While waiting this morning at Swindon station for a train which was 20 minutes late (all the way from Paddington), it occurred to me that the only country left in Europe where trains still run on time is Switzerland.

Is it a coincidence that Switzerland is not a member of the EU?

David Mackintosh
Shrivenham, Wiltshire

14 MARCH 1997

SIR – David Mackintosh (letter, March 13) may like to consider the following paragraph which appeared in the February 1997 issue of the magazine *Today's Railways*: 'Swiss Federal Railways headquarters has ordered stern action against late running after the situation deteriorated to an unacceptable level at the end of 1996. The situation was worst in Biel/Bienne where only 54 per cent were exactly on time and 83 per cent within four minutes of time. SBB's own targets are 75 per cent and 95 per cent.'

Another myth laid to rest?

Michael Dean
Kettering, Northants.

19 MARCH 1997

SIR – The Swiss railway system is worse than Michael Dean states (letter, March 14). As a regular commuter from Tannay to Geneva, I recorded train times during December and January.

Of the 25 train journeys I took during this period, only two were on time and the average delay for trains arriving at Tannay was seven minutes. This makes British Rail look positively efficient and the potential advantages of Switzerland joining the European Union considerable if the Swiss Federal Railways noted the standards of their potential European partners.

Peter Rees-Gildea
Vaud, Switzerland

24 MARCH 1997

SIR – We have been following with interest, and not a little indignation, the correspondence about timekeeping on Swiss railways. We have travelled extensively in Switzerland, always using public transport, and found that, in general, their timekeeping is excellent. In large parts of the network (which is not just the Swiss Federal System but also many private standard and narrow-gauge railways), many lines are single track with passing places, so the system would collapse if timekeeping was not adhered to accurately. To compare this with 'efficiency' on British Rail is truly amazing. Even before privatisation, British Rail would not have considered a train which arrived at its destination seven minutes after the advertised arrival time to be late – hence the notorious BR 70 minutes to the hour!

The other ruse widely employed by BR (and not yet corrected by privatised railway companies) was to extend journey times so that trains could be announced as arriving early – a particular example which springs to mind is the Saturday service from Hereford to Paddington, which used to take 2¾ hours and now officially takes 3¼ hours!

Leave the Swiss railway system alone – many of the railway companies traverse terrain unknown in this country, and they really do operate an integrated transport system which is the envy of the world.

Dr & Mrs P.M. Williams

30 JULY 1997
JUST THE TICKET

SIR — Reading your article concerning the use of paid volunteer passengers as guards on commuter trains into London (report, July 26), I observe that the suggestion was received by Jimmy Knapp as one would expect. He describes it as 'the most bizarre proposal in 40 years'.

In 1957 — 40 years ago — I commuted for three weeks from Long Island to New York City, using the Long Island Railroad. All early-morning and evening trains were staffed by commuter conductor/guards, who not only gave the 'right-away' signal but also examined a random number of tickets.

Just because the Secretary of the National Union of Rail, Maritime and Transport Workers is not prepared to carry out research into suggestions of this nature, why do they have to be dismissed as 'bizarre'?

R. Tostevin
Yeovil, Somerset

7 AUG 1997
OUR TRAINS ARE ON THE RIGHT TRACK

SIR — Setting up companies from scratch can often be much easier than taking on established companies — that can be particularly so when it's part of the old British Rail network (Letters, Aug. 4, 5).

When Virgin Rail took over the West Coast main line and Cross Country, we said it would take four years (and the delivery of our tilting trains) before we could say we had created the best rail network in Europe. We are three months into that process and have had our fair share of inherited teething problems: antiquated rolling stock resulting in hopeless air conditioning and run-down lavatories; inadequate staffing levels on phone lines; lack of co-ordination between stations for disabled passengers; wholly inadequate catering structures; late delivery of equipment and so on.

Having said that, we are beginning to see the light at the end of what could have been a very long tunnel. Punctuality, performance and catering have been improved, cancellations reduced, and we are nearly up to full staff on the phone lines. Another two months should see us clear of the worst of the smaller problems, although it will be still some time before we can be truly proud of the transformation. We have committed to invest £800 million in new rolling stock and, with Railtrack, £1.5 billion on infrastructure improvements on the West Coast main line, and a host of other initiatives over the next four years.

In the meantime my personal apologies to anyone who has difficulties. What I can assure you is that we have inherited an excellent team at Virgin Rail, and they are working very hard to get it right.

Richard Branson
Necker Island
British Virgin Islands

9 AUGUST 1997

SIR – It was nice of Richard Branson to write to you (letter, Aug. 7) in defence of Virgin Rail. Twice recently I have written to him c/o his organisation(s); on Wednesday I tried to telephone his 'Customer Relations Team' at Birmingham, in each case without success. As with every multinational and conglomerate company nowadays, the buck gets passed . . .

and passed . . . And, of course, I'm not in the least important, am I?

J.D. Warmingham
Pencoed, Mid-Glamorgan

SIR – Delayed, for the second time this week, by a defective
locomotive, I am beginning to wonder what the difference
might be between today's unreliable and run-down Virgin
Rail and bad old InterCity West Coast. When Mr Branson
returns from the Caribbean, he should perhaps see for
himself what it's like to slum it on one of his trains.

Jeremy Hayes
Water Orton, Birmingham

2 JANUARY 1998
MYTH MEETS ITS WATERLOO

SIR – Is it possible to nail the myth that anyone in Europe
cares a toss that Waterloo is Britain's rail gateway to the
Continent (report, Dec. 31)? Thousands of French and
other Europeans arrive each week at Nicholas Grimshaw's
magnificent steel and glass international station, which, if it
could only be seen from across the Thames, would be widely
acknowledged as a masterpiece of British architecture.

Nobody to the east of France worries about arriving in
Paris at the Gare d'Austerlitz, named after Napoleon's
greatest victory.

Denis MacShane MP (Lab)
London, SW1

23 JANUARY 1998
DEPARTED DOOM

SIR – All has not been downhill since rail privatisation. As your train climbed out of Euston in BR days there used to be a large hoarding beside the line which proclaimed: 'Prepare to meet thy doom.' It is no longer there.

Bill Fay
Berkswell, Warwickshire

3 OCTOBER 1998
BAD OLD DAYS ON THE RAILWAYS

SIR – Am I alone in enjoying the delicious irony of seeing Labour getting all steamed up over the railways and the delays that their poor delegates have suffered? How many thousands recall the good old days when the unions and their Labour lap-dogs wreaked merry hell on the travelling public?

They used to choose either the hottest months or the coldest for their action. For weeks we would suffer Wednesday strikes, or better still a Tuesday and Thursday combination which caused even more disruption. However, we were always greatly comforted by the knowledge that they were never carried out to inconvenience the passengers – merely to bring their demands to our attention.

It is not hard to see why there are more complaints now that privatisation has occurred. It is because these companies are now subjected to real accountability: they have to listen to and react to complaints.

Philip Coulson
Faversham, Kent

SIR – As one who, for 30 years, commuted daily 25 miles to Waterloo, I am able to state categorically that today's travellers do not know what real difficulties are. Through the 1960s and 1970s, British Rail was governed by the likes of 'Red' Ray Buckton and dear Sid Greene. One was extremely lucky if just a tenth of a week's journeys saw the destination reached on time. But by far the most horrendous occasions involved going to Waterloo in the evening to find that a full-blown strike had started during the day. If it was not the train drivers, it was the guards. If it was not the guards, it was the signal-box men, and so on – but, of course, it was never to hurt the travelling public. Commuters then had the problem of trying to find a bed for the night or spending the darkness hours at the termini. The financial cost and disruption to family life were tremendous.

John Prescott could do something useful by reimbursing those who suffered so much at the hands of his trade union comrades during the days of the grossly inefficient, heavily subsidised British Rail – many thousands of pounds each at today's prices.

Edward Preston
Havant, Hampshire

21 OCTOBER 1998
SIGNAL FAILURES

SIR – In view of the recent failures by privatised rail companies to deliver either their commitments or their passengers, perhaps they now deserve the treatment traditionally meted out to airline acronyms. (Sabena: Such A Bad Experience, Never Again; TWA: Try Walking Across).

I suggest: Connex: Can't Operate Network, No Expertise; Virgin: Very Irate Riders Get In Never; Railtrack: Really Awful Infrastructure, Lines Too Rusty And Coaches Kaput; and GNER: Going Nowhere, Even Reverse.

David Freedman
Berkhamsted, Herts.

8 OCTOBER 1999
WHAT NEEDS TO BE DONE AFTER THE CRASH

SIR – As a survivor of the Paddington crash, I would like to suggest some measures that would improve safety. I was in the second carriage of the train from Gloucester, which turned on its side.

One of the left-hand windows smashed in the impact, and many of us climbed out through it. But climbing up through what is effectively a hole in the ceiling lined with broken glass is difficult for fit people.

It is nearly impossible for elderly or the injured. All high-speed train carriages, therefore, should be fitted with emergency exits in the roof.

A colleague sitting further along the carriage attempted to break the sliding glass doors with the hammer provided, but the hammer broke. These hammers should be replaced.

The emergency services arrived at the scene quite quickly, but the sight of the seriously injured having to sit by the side of the track while security services cut through an eight-foot-high steel security fence was harrowing.

All sections of busy multi-line track near main termini should have an access road alongside for emergency vehicles.

Of course trains should have seat belts. We accept them in

planes and cars, so why not trains? I was lucky to be thrown into a table, only badly bruising my chest.

Tony Cima
The Camp, Glos.

SIR — As a Railtrack shareholder, I found its six-monthly report for shareholders, Railtalk, painfully illuminating.

The preface has a cartoon of a grinning mouth and highlights 'performance' and 'investment'. In four paragraphs, there is no mention of safety. Page two has seven paragraphs entitled 'Around the network' with no mention of safety. Page three is from a statement by chairman Sir Robert Horton to the 1999 AGM saying 'performance is always the top of Railtrack's agenda. . .'; no mention of safety in eight paragraphs.

Page four lists the top 10 issues raised by shareholders: none mentions safety. Safety is mentioned just once. Page five reports a conversation with Gerald Corbett, Railtrack chief executive, saying: 'Our main objective is to deliver a safe railway . . . the safety record of the railway has been steadily improving over the last five years . . .'

Peter West
Ilkley, West Yorks.

SIR — Three days after the disaster, many people will have received their Railtrack half-yearly share dividends. I invite everyone who has received a dividend to follow my example and donate the total sum to the disaster fund when it is opened.

I would expect Railtrack, without prejudice, to donate a sum equal to that given by the shareholders.

Captain M.S. Moreton
Paddock Wood, Kent

SIR – Is it coincidence that the worst railway accidents on this stretch of westerly-bound line have happened at rush hour in the autumn?

Driving my children to school at 8.10 yesterday morning, I was struck by how difficult it was to see traffic lights in the low morning sunlight. Is it possible the train driver out of Paddington had the same problem, as the low, easterly rising sun shone full on the west-bound signals?

Jane Brown
Purley, Surrey

SIR – Notwithstanding the common sense of having automatic stopping systems, the fact that a driver can miss a red light at all suggests that the lights are not bright enough. If we can see emergency service vehicles with high intensity pulsating lights over great distances even in daylight, why are similar red lights not employed on the railways?

Stephen Meadows
Haslemere, Surrey

SIR – Your diagram on page five shows that there is no safety net for the train to prevent it physically from running on to the main line.

It might have been deflected onto the down line (track four) had it been spotted in the control centre, but this may have been prevented by interlocks once it was on the track circuit. Politicians and experts alike are all chasing after the perfect safety system. There is no such thing, but our grandparents used the simple expedient of a set of points which ran an offending train off the subsidiary line, into a sand trap which brought it to a rapid if sudden halt somewhere where it did not impinge on passing traffic.

An embarrassment for the driver, but no lives lost. All drivers (in my experience) become acutely aware of such traps and know they must be sure the road is set before running foul of them. One seldom hears of overruns where they still exist.

It is apparent from the alterations I have noted over the past 20 years that signal engineers are so confident of their ability to control trains that they have gone away from the first principle of rail safety, namely physical separation. One argument is undoubtedly cost; however, the death toll in this accident can be directly attributed to a design engineer who saved about £18,000 by not replacing the trap which must once have been there.

There should be an immediate review of layouts of the 600 reported overrun incidents (an appalling admission of failure) and a conscious decision taken now to reinstall trap points in every location where the train might have caused a collision on a converging track. Had there been a sand trap at each end of the single line section, the recent accident in Kent where two trains met head on could not physically have happened, fog or no fog.

Lt-Col David Pagan
Camberley, Surrey

SIR — The time has come for the people who direct and supervise the rail system to demonstrate their commitment to safety.

Every director, both executive and non-executive, and every manager, irrespective of function, should be mandated to spend not less than four hours per month, minimum journey time two hours, in the driver's cab of a train, selected on a random basis.

David Rowles
Highnam, Glos.

4 DECEMBER 1999
FRESH MEMORIES

SIR – At 7.35 p.m. on Wednesday, December 1, I called National Rail Enquiries to be greeted by a recorded message informing me that my call was unable to be answered so as to allow staff the opportunity of observing the Armistice Day silence. I needed two minutes to recover.

Andrew Chatburn
Maidstone, Kent

3 NOVEMBER 2000
WORSE THAN BR

SIR – As a long-suffering commuter on Connex trains, I was somewhat bemused by Gerald Corbett's comment that 'train punctuality will have to take a back seat for the next two years' (report, Nov. 2). Unfortunately, Mr Corbett, it has taken a back seat for many years now.

Time-keeping was bad under British Rail, but it was a vast improvement on today's standards.

Ian Fossey
Bexhill-on-Sea, E. Sussex

30 APRIL 2001
NUMBERS GAME

SIR – Your prediction (leading article, Apr. 28) that lengthy train journeys over the weekend would be mercifully quiet because of confusion over the switch to new mobile telephone numbers was more hopeful than accurate. After 40 minutes on a train to Birmingham from London, I had to change seats to escape the noise of a thoughtless young man in a seat behind me incessantly phoning friends 'just to make sure you have the new number'. Is there no escape?

Mrs Jenny Thornton
London, SW2

4 JANUARY 2002
RAILWAYS MUST BE RENATIONALISED

SIR – David Graves states that Gavin Strang, the transport minister in 1997, said that privatisation of the railways by the Tories had failed and 'continued to fail' (report, Jan. 1).

The railways were nationalised to become a public service by the Transport Act 1947 and ran for 50 years with greater success as a public service than their privately owned predecessors, GWR, LMS, LNER and SR. While, surely, few would deny Mr Strang's conclusion that privatisation has failed (and failed miserably), an even greater error of judgement has been the failure of the Labour Government in preferring to tinker with a hopelessly failed enterprise in lieu of renationalisation.

It seems incredible that the politicians cannot devise a scheme that would provide the finance for renationalising this national asset in terms that would provide a reasonable return on the investment to the Government by way of interest.

Peter Carter-Ruck
Bishop's Stortford, Herts.

5 JANUARY 2002

SIR – I don't know where Peter Carter-Ruck (letter, Jan. 4) was during the 50 years of nationalised British Rail, but I bet he never suffered the exquisite torture it inflicted on the long-suffering public. I defy him to cite a single aspect of rail operation that was better under nationalisation. If he wants one reason why most of us wouldn't travel by rail, even to our own funerals, it is a memory of the shuddering horror of nationalised British Snail.

The reason John Major's timid Tories privatised the railways is the same as the reason Labour will not renationalise them: namely the need, under the terms of the Maastricht Treaty, to get the massive investment needed to undo 50 years of neglect off the public books. This was necessary in order to meet the criteria for public-sector debt set out in that treaty.

John Hay-Heddle
Long Eaton, Notts.

11 JANUARY 2002
THE TORTOISE

SIR – If South West Trains' dispute with Greg Tucker of the RMT is about him driving too fast (report, Jan. 6), I have a solution that may be acceptable to both parties.

Mr Tucker should be reinstated as a driver and given the

Dorking to Waterloo route. Today's journey averaged a sedate 14 m.p.h., even though we stopped at only half the stations that we were supposed to visit.

This is not a one-off occurrence — we are regularly overtaken by invalid carriages, people walking their dogs and once by an old lady in a wheelchair.

I wonder if any other readers get a similarly leisurely ride into work courtesy of South West Trains and Railtrack.

David Pollard
Westhumble, Surrey

SIR — Can we really expect Tony Blair to be that bothered about the railways, when an anagram of his name is 'Not By Rail'?

Charles Stacey
St Osyth, Essex

14 JANUARY 2002
MUZAK ATTACK

SIR — Having been driven out of countless public places by over-amplified pop music, I was delighted to learn that vandals are being driven out of our railway stations by classical music (report, Jan. 12).

As a frequent long-distance rail traveller, could I exhort stations on Virgin Trains' routes to introduce Wagner? During an average journey, it should be possible for opera lovers to fit in the whole of *Das Rheingold* and perhaps the first act of *Die Walkure* as well. Free, quality entertainment in decent surroundings — what bliss.

Judith Payne
Berwick-upon-Tweed, Northumberland

16 JANUARY 2002

SIR – As well as playing Wagner on train journeys (letter, Jan. 14), perhaps we could also give some of the *Nibelung* hordes a job with Railtrack, where they could get their little hammers out and mend some of the cracked rails.

Geoff Wright
Doncaster

16 JANUARY 2002

A PUNCTUAL CONTROLLER

SIR – Perhaps we could learn a little about punctuality from a former chairman of the Great Eastern Railway until 1895, my great-grandfather Charles Henry Parkes.

He was known as Punctuality Parkes, and it was his practice to have a chair carried on to the footbridge at Liverpool Street Station. He would sit with his gold hunter watch in his hand and watch the arrival and departure of trains.

If a train arrived late, he would send for the driver and ask him the reason; if it was the driver's fault, he would be reprimanded, but if it was due to a mechanical or signalling fault, the appropriate engineer would be sent for and told to correct the problem. I am told that, after six months of this regime, lateness on the GER was almost unheard of.

Perhaps Stephen Byers could have a chair at Waterloo and Tony Blair at Paddington for a trial period.

Richard Parkes
Kingswear, Devon

22 JANUARY 2002
INHUMANE TREATMENT

SIR — It is touching that Tony Blair's Government is so concerned by the plight of British al-Qa'eda terrorists that it should send envoys to Cuba to ensure that they are treated humanely.

I wonder when Mr Blair will send envoys to sit on our trains to ensure that commuters are also treated humanely?

Robert Davies
Robertsbridge, E. Sussex

7 FEBRUARY 2002
TRAINS PAY

SIR — My late father was an ASLEF driver from 1917 to 1968, and never wanted his sons to follow him. As a result of scholarships I became a university lecturer and my brother a university vice-chancellor. With the revelation that drivers now get professional salaries, if I had sons I would be advising them to follow their grandfather instead of their father.

Dr Ken Mason
Loughborough, Leics.

2 AUGUST 2002
OUTSIDE HELP

SIR — I have a suggestion for Connex (report, Aug. 1). To ease overcrowding in trains why not fit straps on the outside of your carriages as well, so that passengers can hang on and run alongside, as footmen did in the old days of the nobility?

Alan Cresswell
Ilminster, Somerset

3 AUGUST 2002

SIR — Alan Cresswell's suggestion that Connex trains be fitted with outside straps so passengers can run alongside (Letters, Aug. 2) is ridiculous. The trains don't go fast enough to keep up.

Mike Cazalet
Narborough, Leics.

14 AUGUST 2002
DON'T PHONE HOME

SIR — The suggestion by W.F. Deedes that there should be separate carriages for mobile phone users is already in place on Great Western trains. In practice, few users take much notice of the signs, and 'customer service hosts' and 'on-board conductors' usually have more pressing, Railtrack-related problems to deal with.

Jeremy Deedes
Newbury, Berks

16 AUGUST 2002

SIR — We all hate mobile phone users, even if we are one ourselves (Notebook, Aug. 14). As a solution to this problem, I bought a credit card-sized mobile phone jammer from an Internet site for £20 (alas, now discontinued) and now silence is just the press of a button away.

I find myself hunting mobile users on trains rather than avoiding them. Game on.

Alastair Brent
Fetcham, Surrey

20 AUGUST 2002

SIR — Alastair Brent (Letters, Aug. 16) may enjoy 'hunting mobile phone users on trains' with his jammer, but he should understand that the use of jammers is illegal. If users on trains annoy him, he should ask them to stop.

The mobile operators have paid for exclusive use of those airwaves (over £4 billion for third-generation licences). Indiscriminate use of jammers may also disconnect someone on a genuine emergency call or interfere with other safety-critical radio systems.

I do not like motorways, but I assume there would be objections if I parked a double-decker bus across the M1 to jam it.

Tom Wills-Sandford
Director, Information and Communications Technology
London, SW6

SIR – W.F. Deedes might try my husband's – usually successful – gambit (Notebook, Aug. 12). He leans over the offender and asks him if the person at the other end of the phone would kindly speak loudly as well, so that everyone else in the carriage may join in the conversation.

Pamela Page
East Hagbourne, Oxon.

2 SEPTEMBER 2002
GINGERED UP

SIR – I recently travelled on a train from Kemble to Paddington. In the buffet car I saw this message written on a paper napkin: 'Would the last person on duty tonight please moisten the ginger cake as it is past its sell-by date.'

Kyrle Arscott
Ashton Keynes, Wiltshire

2 OCTOBER 2002
SHAGGY DOG STORY

SIR – While I was travelling from London to Manchester by train on Monday, a dog approximately the size of a small rabbit leapt vertically three feet into the air and sank its teeth into my backside. We remained conjoined in this manner for a number of seconds, to the amusement of my fellow travellers.

The elderly owner explained that this unprovoked behaviour was due to the animal's profound deafness – an excuse which, I'm sure you will agree, is far more believable than those emanating from Virgin West Coast public address systems.

Dr Michael Platten
Manchester

4 OCTOBER 2002

SIR – Dr Michael Platten's shaggy dog story (letter, Oct. 2) reminds me of the heady days of rail travel when one was closeted in close proximity with five other passengers in a first-class corridor compartment.

On one occasion, we were joined by an elderly lady carrying a Pekingese, which, immediately after the train left the station, started yapping and whining continuously. After this irritation had continued for some time, the lady said: 'I'm sorry about this; I don't know what to make of him.'

A disgruntled male voice emanating from behind a newspaper in a far corner seat intoned: 'Why not try a fireside rug, madam?'

Roderick Page
Sandwich, Kent

25 OCTOBER 2002
FASCINATING HOBBY

SIR – I am a model railway enthusiast specialising in the Swanage Railway. In a recent radio programme trailer, I was sorry to hear a trainspotter, who owned a model railway, portrayed as socially inept when dating a woman. I am astonished that such a harmless, creative and fulfilling hobby has become the butt of mindless jokes from the media.

Trainspotting began during the Second World War, when Ian Allan produced a pocket-size book called *Southern Locomotives*, which was a complete list of all the 1,850 Southern locomotives in service in 1942. This eventually included all the locomotives in service on British Railways and was updated each year. The information gained from people who used this book to collect engine numbers has been a valuable source of information for authors and railway modellers.

People who build and run model railway layouts are as far removed from the media's image as it is possible to be. West Wittering Model Railway Circle produced a beautiful model of Swanage Station. The builders included a doctor and his family, a leading author, a teacher and an engineer.

The model did not only authentically recreate the trains and the railway buildings: it was a three-dimensional picture of what life was like in Swanage in the early 1960s. It included Court Hill, the laundry behind Gilbert Hall and the garage that stood on the site of the Post Office. About 10 years ago, we exhibited it in the Caxton Hall in Victoria Street.

I cannot understand why people who have worked so hard to provide so much enjoyment for themselves and others should be subjected to such facile comments from the media.

Robin Brasher
Swanage, Dorset

29 OCTOBER 2002

SIR – I agree with everything Robin Brasher says except for his claim that 'train spotting began during the Second World War' (letter, Oct. 25).

I am a member of a rare breed – a female railway enthusiast – and I was train spotting as early as 1935 (as did my family before me). There were no Ian Allan books then; we produced our own stock books. As I was only four in 1935, I put my later affinity with numbers and a career as a maths teacher down to all those numbers I had to record.

Susan Youell
Leeds

'30 OCTOBER 2002

SIR – Trainspotters have been around since the 1890s, when the Railway Club was founded, not the Second World War (letter, Oct. 25). About that time, G.A. Sekon, for whom my mother worked briefly 85 years ago, founded the *Railway Magazine*. The Railway Correspondence and Travel Society was founded in 1929. With other railway societies, it continues to flourish. Ian Allan seized on already widespread interest to give the average enthusiasts what they wanted in pocket form.

In more recent years, railway enthusiasts have rescued branch lines and steam trains from oblivion, and founded transport museums; they preserve historic engineering and woodworking crafts. Their efforts are now a useful part of heritage and the tourist industry.

Some of us have devoted our energies to the consumer movement, providing expertise, at no fee, that counters the efforts of railway managers to pull the wool over the eyes of rail passengers' consultative committee members.

Railway enthusiasts are at this moment voting for Brunel, railway engineer, as a Great Briton. As for being socially inept, well so can gardeners, hill walkers and stamp collectors be. But is that worse than being the opposite — Costa del Sangria tourists, party ravers and viewers of *Fame Academy*?

Laurie Mack
Bromley, Kent

11 NOVEMBER 2002
SARDINE EXPERIENCE

SIR — As I sat at my desk last week, after another cramped and hot train ride, I found myself considering what future generations will make of how we travel today. More than likely, children visiting the Science Museum in 100 years' time will be able to 'experience' a London commuter journey into work.

I imagine it to function something like this: groups of 100 at a time will be ushered on to a replica London train station platform by surly, unco-operative individuals in badly worn uniforms. They will then be forced to wait for 20 minutes, while being lashed with rain and listening to announcements on a public address system. Needless to say, it will sound like the speaker has a scarf stuffed in his mouth.

The group will then rush towards a set of false train doors, which will attempt to close before they are all safely in. Once inside, there will be no seats available, as these will be occupied by individuals who have the air of never actually having left the train. Then the temperature will be turned up to unbearable levels, leaving them exasperated and hot.

The final touch will be that on any given day, with little or no warning, the ride will not work at all.

Charles Blake Thomas
Twickenham, Richmond

2 JANUARY 2006
ROOM FOR MORE ON TOP?

SIR — I refer to the article by your transport correspondent (Dec. 30) regarding double-decker trains, and the probability that they will first be seen on the Channel Tunnel rail link.

I can remember travelling on one of these trains, in 1955, on my journeys to and from school, on what was then the Dartford Loop line. Admittedly, there was not much headroom when one was seated upstairs, but no alterations were needed to the railway infrastructure.

Perhaps it is time to dust down the original plans, and update them as necessary.

A.R. Johnson
Calne, Wiltshire

4 JANUARY 2006

SIR — Like A.R. Johnson (Letters, Jan. 2), I travelled on the Southern Region's double-decker trains on the Dartford line in the 1950s.

As I recall, these trains were withdrawn after relatively short service on what was, and remains, an intensive and crowded commuter system, on the grounds that loading and de-training passengers at the frequent intermediate stops created timekeeping delays.

The problem was simply that since upstairs and downstairs passengers used the same door to get on and off, it took at least half as long again to effect entry and exit.

Similar trains seem to be used successfully on French suburban lines today, and, of course, on a non-stop route such as the Channel Tunnel Rail Link, the problem would occur only at either end of the line.

Martin Hall
Erith, Kent

5 JANUARY 2006

SIR – The double-deck railway carriages that took too long to load and unload (Letters, Jan. 4) were designed at the behest of the chief mechanical engineer of the Southern Railway before it was nationalised. Unfortunately, they had to operate within the restrictive loading gauge of that railway. That is the profile of vehicles that can travel on a particular line, and specifies their height and width and includes cut-outs to clear platform edges, etc.

Double-deck carriages are used successfully on overseas railways that have the necessarily generous loading gauge, such as in Sydney. The bad news for British commuters is that these carriages will require a massive programme of track-side widening, enlarging tunnel profiles and the raising of bridges. This work would depend upon the availability of funds and a change in culture among the politicians and bureaucrats who run our transport infrastructure. The only cost-effective way to raise capacity on suburban lines would be to increase the length of trains with extra carriages and to provide longer platforms to accommodate them.

W.D. Toulman
Walkington, E. Yorkshire

14 FEBRUARY 2006

SIR – When I arrive at Victoria Station by train, I make a point of thanking the train driver if I see him.

Mark you, I sometimes wonder, from the surprised expression on his face, if he thinks I am swearing at him.

P.C. McCoy
Cobham, Kent

10 JUNE 2006
NO BARRIER TO VANDALS

SIR – While I applaud the Transport Secretary's intention to test anti-terrorism barriers at Victoria and Waterloo stations (report, June 7), I wonder why it is that we are unable to deter or detect most of the graffiti vandals who invade our rail networks and rolling stock every night.

Bob Bryan
Teddington, Middlesex

22 JUNE 2006
READING OUT LOUD

SIR – In response to your correspondent (June 20) who was forced to listen to noisy mobile phone conversations in public places, I have often wondered what would be the reaction if I were to read my newspaper out aloud on the train. I have never had the courage to do it, though.

Robert Curtis
Writtle, Essex

24 JUNE 2006

SIR – Robert Curtis (Letters, June 22) says that he does not have the courage to read his newspaper aloud in retaliation against mobile phones.

Perhaps he should take lessons on a brass instrument. The late musician Dennis Brain is said to have asked a fellow train passenger to turn off his radio. When his request was refused, he took out his French horn and started to practise.

Ron Sloggett
Fleet, Hants

SIR – I did read out loud, and it worked a treat. The culprit took it in good part, and we chatted amicably all the way to Victoria.

Betty Mulcahy
Brighton, E. Sussex

SIR – I have not tried reading my newspaper out loud on a train, but, several years ago, I read some chapters from an Enid Blyton *Secret Seven* book to my children on a train between Malvern and Reading, having decided that it was preferable to putting up with two very fidgety, bored children.

A number of passengers around me appeared to be listening with interest, no doubt reviving childhood memories.

Valerie Fane
Malvern, Worcs.

SIR – Forget about the frown, the sharp intake of breath or the irritable toss of the head. Instead, join in, listen overtly and eagerly, nodding, smiling and occasionally tilting the head or cupping the ear. At all times, you should look interested and anxious to hear every word.

If the speaker turns away in order to gain some privacy, you should try to move, too. It is also vital to try to maintain constant eye contact with him or her. I usually find the call is brought to an abrupt end.

Susan Cokyll
London, NW1

6 FEBRUARY 2008
TRYING TO LOCATE EBBSFLEET INTERNATIONAL STATION

SIR – After reading that Ebbsfleet International station is a new stop on the line linking St Pancras to Europe (report, Jan. 30), I thought I would find out where it is. My British road atlas did not list it, and on the web neither Google nor the AA route map mentioned it.

When I telephoned the AA it could not help, and in the end I telephoned National Rail Enquiries. I was told that Ebbsfleet was close to Dartford. I remarked that I could not find it on any map, only to be told: 'Oh, it does not exist yet. It is just a muddy field!'

John Cetti
Barnet, Hertfordshire

15 JANUARY 2010

FLEETING DELIGHT OF A SCENE FRAMED BY A TRAIN WINDOW

SIR – Charles Spencer (Features, Jan. 11) invites readers to suggest delights of winter. Mine are sights of Britain from a railway compartment, which suits the weather – as long as the heating works and the snow has not stopped the train.

I have in mind sights such as Lincoln, Rochester and Durham cathedrals, approached by rail. Since they are framed for only a limited time, the impact is intense. The panorama from a train window beats anything visible from a car, which usually delivers little more than the sight of a motorway embankment.

Rupert Nicholson
Shipley, West Yorkshire

10 FEBRUARY 2010

THE QUEEN COMMUTING

SIR – While I am pleased to see the Queen apparently using public transport at King's Lynn station (report, Feb. 9), was she really 'among commuters'? If she was, I wonder if she was still smiling on arrival in London – given the failure of so many trains to run on time and the indignity of having to stand in a crowded carriage.

David J. Waring
Grappenhall, Cheshire

26 APRIL 2010
RENATIONALISED RAILWAYS

SIR – With the acquisition of Arriva (report, April 22) by Deutsche Bahn, which already owns or runs EWS (operator of the royal train), London Overground, Tyneside Metro, Wrexham & Shropshire and Chiltern Rail, it seems those that wish to see our trains returned to state ownership can start to celebrate.

I would personally have preferred it had the state in question been Britain, but perhaps we can at least look forward to improved efficiency on Arriva services.

John Vance
Kingsdown, Kent

29 APRIL 2010
OVERCROWDED NEW TRAINS

SIR – The new carriages on First Capital Connect are a glaring exception to the rule that products get better over time. The old ones dealt quite well with the demands of crowded journeys. They provided those forced to stand a choice of handles and rails to grip.

The replacement carriages lack these proven basics. Now, people have to try to grab the edge of the luggage rack. The hooped grips on seats have become solid semi-circles of plastic, which have to be pinched between thumb and fingers.

But the most incompetent aspect of the redesign is the inter-carriage doors. They are now opened by a proximity sensor, instead of a handle. When the carriage is crowded, passengers lean against the wall adjacent to the sliding door, which apparently can't cope with a nearly stationary body on the fringe of its zone. For the duration of a recent 25-minute journey I was treated to dozens of phantom door openings.

In many industries, it is standard practice to test designs before production. Did the designers of this abomination never think to test a commuter carriage with people standing?

Geoff Lacey
Harpenden, Hertfordshire

21 OCTOBER 2010
TEA CADDY SAVES THE DAY

SIR — Last Friday, I travelled by train from Birmingham to Cheltenham. Asking for a cup of tea at the buffet, I was told that I could not have one as they had no paper bag to put the cup in; I was not permitted to carry a cup back to my seat in the next carriage. 'Health and safety,' they said.

The train guard happened to be there and offered to help. So I returned to my seat, closely followed by the guard, who carried my tea.

Tore Fauske
Woodmancote, Gloucestershire

2 NOVEMBER 2010
NAILING BAD BEHAVIOUR

SIR — Returning from work recently by train, I had my attention drawn by a loud clicking noise. On looking up, I saw a well-dressed man sitting across the aisle clipping his fingernails.

Could your readers suggest how one might display appropriate outrage at such behaviour?

Andrew Hall
Thakeham, West Sussex

4 NOVEMBER 2010

SIR – The appropriate way to respond to a fellow passenger clipping his fingernails on the train (Letters, Nov. 2) is to ask: 'Would you like me to do your toenails?'

Dr Bill Costello
Tibenham, Norfolk

SIR – Pick imaginary pieces of nail from the floor and deposit them on his lap, preferably wearing gloves.

Sandy Pratt
Lingfield, Surrey

SIR – On the train from Leeds to Sheffield every day, my wife sees a chap who brings out an electric shaver, does the deed and empties the contents on to the floor.

Ian Robinson
Leeds, West Yorkshire

14 DECEMBER 2010

WARMING UP ON A TRAIN

SIR – In the days before train heating (Letters, Dec. 13), the Irish Mail – a train that took post and passengers from Euston

to Holyhead, where the mail could be put on a ship –
introduced the use of sacks of mixed chemical salts, which
reacted to produce heat, to put under passengers' feet in
winter.

As time passed, the reaction needed reactivating and when
the train stopped at stations, porters would enter the
compartments to shake the sacks. The general kerfuffle
caused passengers to start conversations and gave rise to the
social expression 'breaking the ice'.

Roger Croston
Chester

21 DECEMBER 2010
FAST RAIL ADVANTAGES

SIR – I much enjoyed reading Andrew Gilligan's article
(Comment, Dec. 20) on HS2, the proposed high speed rail
route – as a polemic. But perhaps he omitted some of the
facts.

The West Coast and East Coast main lines are almost full.
Since privatisation rail travel has increased by 40 per cent or
more, and extra capacity will soon be needed. It would be
wildly expensive and disruptive to add extra tracks to existing
routes. A new route is a cheaper solution and can be designed
for higher speeds.

The route from London to Birmingham is only the
beginning of a network whose benefits will grow as it extends
north to Manchester and Leeds – and further.

Domestic services on HS1 (the Channel Tunnel rail link)
attract six million passengers a year – a million of whom have
changed from road to rail, according to *Railnews*.

It's right to debate the merits of a new railway line, and to consider carefully the interests of those who are affected. But a visit to the route of HS1 should convince anybody that a rail line is far less intrusive and noisy than a motorway.

James Strachan
Cambridge

SIR – All over Europe I see infrastructure projects that proudly proclaim: 'Built with EU funding'. Why, if part of the HS2 objective is closer links with Europe, does it not receive similar funding?

At least that way, if it's the failure many of us predict, we could blame the EU.

Godfrey Solomon
Sicklinghall, North Yorkshire

23 DECEMBER 2010

HIGH SPEED TWO WILL BE A VITAL ARTERY, AND LESS INTRUSIVE THAN A MOTORWAY

SIR – At last Britain is to invest properly in its railway system, after years of starvation since the nationalisation of 1948. High Speed Two will be a vital artery, particularly once it is extended to Manchester and the North East.

High Speed Two will avoid the necessity of constructing a relief motorway, which would be far more intrusive, producing much higher and continuous noise nuisance, especially at night. An electrified two-track railway requires only a 10-yard-wide trackway, compared with nearly 40 yards for a dual three-lane motorway, which would involve using much more land.

One objection to High Speed Two has been that there will

be no intermediate stations serving the Chilterns, yet it would not be the function of High Speed Two to carry commuter traffic.

It will avoid attracting the strip development which occurred in Hertfordshire and Bedfordshire following the electrification of the Peterborough to London line in the 1980s.

Viaducts and bridges will of course be necessary in some locations, but if carefully designed will enhance the countryside. Some of our famous railway viaducts, such as John Rastrick's magnificent Ouse viaduct, north of Brighton, and the Royal Border bridge, at Berwick-upon-Tweed, are an accepted part of the scene.

Alan Hayward
Fellow, Royal Society of Engineers
Chepstow, Gwent

SIR – It is said that when Russian rail engineers were planning the route between St Petersburg and Moscow, they decided to consult the tsar.

He leant over the map, took a ruler, placed it on a direct line between St Petersburg and Moscow and with all the skill of an unpractised draughtsman, drew a more or less straight line, with a kink round his thumb near the town of Torbino.

The engineers did indeed follow the tsar's suggestion and the kink in the line is there to this day.

I wonder which of the Transport Secretary's 'refinements' will one day be known as Hammond's Thumb?

Michael Osborn
Oundle, Peterborough

SIR — It seems crazy to spend all this money on new track through unspoilt countryside when there are thousands of miles of underused tracks all over Britain.

Surely St Pancras to Sheffield is a line that could be relatively cheaply upgraded to high speed, largely following the existing route as well as undergoing a long-overdue electrification.

At Sheffield, the line would split, with one branch going on to Manchester and another going to Leeds on a new track, but thereafter using the excellent four-track lines to York and Darlington.

Andrew Beveridge
Aberdeen

29 JANUARY 2011

THE CLOSURE OF BRITAIN'S MOST-LIKED RAIL SERVICE

SIR — News that the Wrexham, Shropshire and Marylebone railway is closing down, when it was the most-liked service in Britain, is a blow to those who believe in competition and excellence on the railways.

We must demand to know how Virgin Trains' mono-polistic hold on the West Coast main line forced this brave and unsubsidised outfit to use slow lines and forbade them from picking up passengers at lucrative stations.

By contrast, on the East Coast main line, from King's Cross to Edinburgh, we have nine operators fighting it out, forcing them to find better ways to serve neglected towns and cities.

The Wrexham, Shropshire and Marylebone believed in

giving people proper carriages with seats aligned with big windows, quietly hauled by a loco at the front. It served the best breakfast in Britain at your seat. It was like rail travel as it used to be: a pleasure.

Monopoly companies are increasingly forcing people into ghastly airline-style seating and scrapping dining cars or even buffets; they have ruthlessly destroyed the hundreds of daily services they inherited from British Rail.

These companies can only produce the profits their shareholders and the Treasury demand by having people packed in, often standing, while lines of carriages (some brand new) stand idle or are sold off overseas. In the past, there were always enough carriages.

For this we pay about three times as much as we did for British Rail, which was the cheapest, fastest, safest and least subsidised railway in the world at the time.

It is a scandal on a par with building aircraft carriers with no planes or scrapping billion-pound early warning aircraft that have never flown.

So, why do we have privatised railways but do not encourage competition?

Benedict Le Vay
London, SW19

30 JUNE 2011

HIGH–SPEED RAIL WILL COST JOBS AND HARM BUSINESSES IN SMALL COMMUNITIES

SIR – The argument over high-speed rail has seemingly been reduced to a 'choice' between gardens in the Chilterns or jobs up north (report, June 20). Well, around our small community, the route of High Speed Two (HS2) will cost jobs.

Apart from the farms that it will affect, it is projected to cut through the sites of several businesses. Near to us, a garage, a garden nursery, polo grounds and a computer games manufacturer will be affected, which threatens the livelihoods of scores of people. Compensation? Who's fooled by that? Meanwhile, near Kenilworth it is proposed to cut across Stoneleigh Park, the former site of the Royal Show, which hosts shows and exhibitions and is the headquarters of many agricultural businesses. Obviously the supporters of HS2, who paint objectors as toffs or nimbies, are adopting the maxim: if losing the argument, throw in a red herring.

Malcolm Hayes
Southam, Warwickshire

SIR – The arguments against HS2 centre on the route, the environmental impact, and the inability of those inconvenienced by the route to use the high-speed trains. These are pretty much the same arguments that were hotly debated when the High Speed One route, the Channel Tunnel link from London through Kent, was first mooted.

HS1 is now built, and objections to HS2 from people in Kent are notable by their absence, because the environmental impact is nothing like as bad as is made out by the theorists. There are also many benefits, such as the release of strain on the overused existing network, improved services, and spin-offs such as improved house prices at places now better served.

In the case of HS2, this will mean that the existing West Coast main line will serve interim stations better than it currently can, and will carry more freight. The benefits of high-speed rail — so long as enough electricity is generated for it to be able to run — are enormous, as has been seen in many other countries. Come on, Kent, give us your verdict 10 years on.

Peter Owen
Claygate, Surrey

SIR — Travelling out of Beijing South, Peter Foster reports seeing straw-hatted farmers tilling their fields as rural China flashes by ('Full speed ahead for railway of the future', June 28). The other day I walked along lanes, admiring mist over the Misbourne Valley, while a cloth-capped farmer tended his dairy herd. I should enjoy this view while it lasts — it is the planned route of Britain's high-speed link.

Dominic Owen
Little Missenden, Buckinghamshire

SIR — I long for a high-speed line to Scotland, where my father lives. From London it is quicker to travel by train the 400 miles to Strasbourg than the 330 to Edinburgh. How can we be so far behind?

Anne Keleny
Orpington, Kent

12 JULY 2011

SIR — It's time the high-speed train protesters thought about what has happened in the Thames Valley over the 170 years since railways were introduced, and, in particular, over the last 36 years, when we have had high-speed trains both to

South Wales and to Devon and Cornwall.

Between Reading and Bristol, the high-speed 125s thunder right through the middle of a selection of some of the prettiest villages in Britain and after an initial scare (lasting maybe a week) one really doesn't notice anything untoward. I slept very happily just 150 feet from the South Wales line for five years, and even now, about half a mile from the line, our lives are undisturbed.

High-speed trains have produced a booming house market and excellent industrial growth prospects in urban areas.

Christopher Glover
Streatley, Berkshire

20 AUGUST 2011

RAILWAY WAITING ROOM TRANSFORMED INTO GALLERY

SIR – The waiting room at our station in Chesterfield looked as bleak as your picture of Aberdeen (Letters, Aug. 16) until the Duke of Devonshire lent an interesting and varied selection of paintings (originals, not prints) from Chatsworth.

Their installation considerably brightened the room and, since none has been stolen or defaced, nor any of the glass smashed, continue to do so.

Perhaps owners of other great houses with surplus pictures could follow his excellent example.

Philip Riden
Chesterfield, Derbyshire

SIR – Three cheers for Norman Baker, the transport minister, who has made a plea for rail passengers to be left in peace from announcements (report, Aug. 17).

Why doesn't the rail industry carry out a trial by switching off the announcements in 'quiet carriages'? They would find passengers voting with their seats.

Peter Dilloway
Medstead, Hampshire

SIR – It is a surprise to me that, while rail companies call their passengers 'customers' and trains 'services' they still use the outmoded 'stations' and 'platforms'. Perhaps customers of this newspaper can suggest modern alternatives.

David Harris
Taunton, Somerset

22 AUGUST 2011

MAKING ONESELF UNDERSTOOD IN RAILWAY NEWSPEAK

SIR – David Harris (Letters, Aug. 20) asks what stations and platforms would be called in railway English: can I suggest 'transit hubs' and 'access facilities'?

Cynthia Harrod-Eagles
Northwood, Middlesex

SIR – How about 'Purgatory' and 'Styx'?

Tim Tawney
Hildenborough, Kent

SIR — How about 'Customer Regional Assembly Point' and 'Customer Rallying And Migration Pier'? In the interests of brevity, acronyms could be substituted.

David Brown
Lavenham, Suffolk

SIR — A platform could be a 'stand', a hint as to what the journey ahead may entail.

Ginny Hudson
Swanmore, Hampshire

SIR — I am acquainted with 'station-stop', but I have also contemplated if one's belongings can be anything other than 'personal', if destinations can be anything other than 'final' and whether being 'able to offer no hot water' is even possible.

Matthew Atkinson
Richmond, Surrey

SIR — The idea to call trains 'services' is not new. It was devised by British Rail to change staff attitudes to their 'customers'.

Stations were to be called 'railheads' but, thankfully, this never caught on.

Nick Ratnieks
West Clandon, Surrey

SIR – A platform should be an 'elevated and ramped non-organic customer-rail modal interface facilitation device'.

Iain Harris
Winchester, Hampshire

25 AUGUST 2011

LEAPING ABOARD THE CHARABANC OF WORD SALVAGE

SIR – My favourite train announcement (Letters, Aug. 22) is 'No smoking in the vestibules', which conjures up images of errant clergy huddled between the carriages in their clerical vestments, enveloped in a haze of cigarette smoke.

Howard Jackson
Torquay, Devon

SIR – No announcement is more annoying or useless than that heard repeatedly on the London to Dover Priory/Ramsgate line, before the train divides at Faversham: 'This is coach number 11 of eight.'

Ann Westbrook
Wootton, Kent